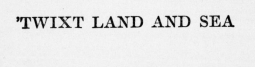

'TWIXT LAND AND SEA

'TWIXT LAND AND SEA

BY
JOSEPH CONRAD

Life is a tragic folly
Let us laugh and be jolly
Away with melancholy
Bring me a branch of holly
Life is a tragic folly.

A. SYMONS.

GARDEN CITY   NEW YORK
DOUBLEDAY, PAGE & COMPANY
1924

TO
CAPTAIN C. M. HARRIS
LATE MASTER AND OWNER
OF THE
ARABY MAID: ARCHIPELAGO TRADER
IN MEMORY OF THOSE
OLD DAYS OF ADVENTURE

AUTHOR'S NOTE

THE only bond between these three stories is, so to speak, geographical, for their scene, be it land, be it sea, is situated in the same region which may be called the region of the Indian Ocean with its off-shoots and prolongations north of the equator even as far as the Gulf of Siam. In point of time they belong to the period immediately after the publication of that novel with the awkward title "Under Western Eyes" and, as far as the life of the writer is concerned, their appearance in a volume marks a definite change in the fortunes of his fiction. For there is no denying the fact that "Under Western Eyes" found no favour in the public eye, whereas the novel called "Chance" which followed "'Twixt Land and Sea" was received on its first appearance by many more readers than any other of my books.

This volume of three tales was also well received, publicly and privately and from a publisher's point of view. This little success was a most timely tonic for my enfeebled bodily frame. For this may indeed be called the book of a man's convalescence, at least as to three-fourths of it; because The Secret Sharer, the middle story, was written much earlier than the other two.

For in truth the memories of "Under Western Eyes" are associated with the memory of a severe illness which seemed to wait like a tiger in the jungle on the turn of a path to jump on me the moment the last words of that novel were written. The memory of an illness is very much like the memory of a nightmare. On emerging from it in a much enfeebled state I was inspired to direct my tottering steps toward the Indian Ocean, a complete change of surroundings and atmosphere from the Lake of Geneva, as nobody would deny. Begun so languidly and with such a fumbling hand that the first twenty pages or more had to be thrown into the waste-paper basket, A Smile of Fortune, the most purely Indian Ocean story of the three, has ended by becoming what the reader will see. I will only say for myself that I have been patted on the back for it by most unexpected people, personally unknown to me, the chief of them of course being the editor of a popular illustrated magazine who published it serially in one mighty instalment. Who will dare say after this that the change of air had not been an immense success?

The origins of the middle story, The Secret Sharer, are quite other. It was written much earlier and was published first in *Harper's Magazine*, during the early part, I think, of 1911. Or perhaps the latter part? My memory on that point is hazy. The basic fact of the tale I had in my possession for a good many years. It was in truth the common possession of the whole fleet of merchant ships trading to India, China, and Australia: a great company the last years of which coincided with my first years on the wider seas. The fact itself happened on board a very distinguished member of it, *Cutty Sark* by name and belonging to Mr. Willis, a notable ship-owner in his day, one of the kind (they are all underground now) who used personally to see his ships start on their voyages to those distant shores where they showed worthily the honoured house-flag of their owner. I am glad I was not too late to get at least one glimpse of Mr. Willis on a very wet and gloomy morning watching from the pier head of the New South Dock one of his clippers starting on a China voyage—an imposing figure of a man under the invariable white hat so well known in the Port of London, waiting till the head of his ship had swung down-stream before giving her a dignified wave of a big gloved hand. For all I know it may have been the *Cutty Sark* herself though certainly not on that fatal voyage. I do not know the date of the occurrence on which the scheme of The Secret Sharer is founded; it came to light and even got into newspapers about the middle eighties, though I had heard of it before, as it were privately, among the officers of the great wool fleet in which my first years in deep water were served. It came to light under circumstances dramatic enough, I think, but which have nothing to do with my story. In the more specially maritime part of my writings this bit of presentation may take its place as one of my two Calm-pieces. For, if there is to be any classification by subjects, I have done two Storm-pieces in "The Nigger of the *Narcissus*" and in "Typhoon"; and two Calm-pieces: this one and "The Shadow Line," a book which belongs to a later period.

Notwithstanding their autobiographical form the above two stories are not the record of personal experience. Their quality, such as it is, depends on something larger if less precise: on the character, vision and sentiment of the first twenty independent years of my life. And the same may be said of the Freya of the Seven Isles. I was considerably abused for writing that story on the ground of its cruelty, both in public prints and in private letters. I remember one from a man in America who was quite furiously angry. He told me with curses and imprecations that I had no right to write such an abominable thing which, he said, had gratuitously and intolerably harrowed his feelings. It was a very interesting letter to read. Impressive too. I carried it for some days in my pocket. Had I the right? The sincerity of the anger impressed me. Had I the right? Had I really sinned as he said or was it only that man's madness? Yet there was a method in his fury. . . . I composed in my mind a violent reply, a reply of mild argument, a reply of lofty detachment; but they never got on paper in the end and I have forgotten their phrasing. The very letter of the angry man has got lost somehow; and nothing remains now but the pages of the story which I cannot recall and would not recall if I could.

But I am glad to think that the two women in this book: Alice, the sullen, passive victim of her fate, and the actively individual Freya, so determined to be the mistress of her own destiny, must have evoked some sympathies because of all my volumes of short stories this was the one for which there was the greatest immediate demand.

1920.   J. C.

CONTENTS

'TWIXT LAND AND SEA

'TWIXT LAND AND SEA

A SMILE OF FORTUNE

EVER since the sun rose I had been looking ahead. The ship glided gently in smooth water. After a sixty days' passage I was anxious to make my landfall, a fertile and beautiful island of the tropics. The more enthusiastic of its inhabitants delight in describing it as the "Pearl of the Ocean." Well, let us call it the "Pearl." It's a good name. A pearl distilling much sweetness upon the world.

This is only a way of telling you that first-rate sugar-cane is grown there. All the population of the Pearl lives for it and by it. Sugar is their daily bread, as it were. And I was coming to them for a cargo of sugar in the hope of the crop having been good and of the freights being high.

Mr. Burns, my chief mate, made out the land first; and very soon I became entranced by this blue, pinnacled apparition, almost transparent against the light of the sky, a mere emanation, the astral body of an island risen to greet me from afar. It is a rare phenomenon, such a sight of the Pearl at sixty miles off. And I wondered half seriously whether it was a good omen, whether what would meet me in that island would be as luckily exceptional as this beautiful, dreamlike vision so very few seamen have been privileged to behold.

But horrid thoughts of business interfered with my

enjoyment of an accomplished passage. I was anxious
for success and I wished, too, to do justice to the flatter-
ing latitude of my owners' instructions contained in one
noble phrase: "We leave it to you to do the best you
can with the ship." . . . All the world being thus
given me for a stage, my abilities appeared to me no
bigger than a pinhead.

Meantime the wind dropped, and Mr. Burns began
to make disagreeable remarks about my usual bad
luck. I believe it was his devotion for me which made
him critically outspoken on every occasion. All the
same, I would not have put up with his humours if it had
not been my lot at one time to nurse him through a
desperate illness at sea. After snatching him out of
the jaws of death, so to speak, it would have been
absurd to throw away such an efficient officer. But
sometimes I wished he would dismiss himself.

We were late in closing in with the land, and had
to anchor outside the harbour till next day. An unpleasant and unrestful night followed. In this roadstead, strange to us both, Burns and I remained on deck
almost all the time. Clouds swirled down the porphyry
crags under which we lay. The rising wind made a
great bullying noise amongst the naked spars, with
interludes of sad moaning. I remarked that we had
been in luck to fetch the anchorage before dark. It
would have been a nasty, anxious night to hang off a
harbour under canvas. But my chief mate was un-
compromising in his attitude.

"Luck, you call it, sir! Ay—our usual luck. The
sort of luck to thank God it's no worse!"

And so he fretted through the dark hours, while I
drew on my fund of philosophy. Ah, but it was an
exasperating, weary, endless night, to be lying at anchor close under that black coast! The agitated water

made snarling sounds all round the ship. At times a wild gust of wind out of a gully high up on the cliffs struck on our rigging a harsh and plaintive note like the wail of a forsaken soul.

I

By half-past seven in the morning, the ship being then inside the harbour at last and moored within a long stone's-throw from the quay, my stock of philosophy was nearly exhausted. I was dressing hurriedly in my cabin when the steward came tripping in with a morning suit over his arm.

Hungry, tired, and depressed, with my head engaged inside a white shirt irritatingly stuck together by too much starch, I desired him peevishly to "heave round with that breakfast." I wanted to get ashore as soon as possible.

"Yes, sir. Ready at eight, sir. There's a gentleman from the shore waiting to speak to you, sir."

This statement was curiously slurred over. I dragged the shirt violently over my head and emerged staring.

"So early!" I cried. "Who's he? What does he want?"

On coming in from sea one has to pick up the conditions of an utterly unrelated existence. Every little event at first has the peculiar emphasis of novelty. I was greatly surprised by that early caller; but there was no reason for my steward to look so particularly foolish.

"Didn't you ask for the name?" I inquired in a stern tone.

"His name's Jacobus, I believe," he mumbled shamefacedly.

"Mr. Jacobus!" I exclaimed loudly, more surprised

than ever, but with a total change of feeling. "Why couldn't you say so at once?"

But the fellow had scuttled out of my room. Through the momentarily opened door I had a glimpse of a tall, stout man standing in the cuddy by the table on which the cloth was already laid; a "harbour" table cloth, stainless and dazzlingly white. So far good.

I shouted courteously through the closed door, that I was dressing and would be with him in a moment. In return the assurance that there was no hurry reached me in the visitor's deep, quiet undertone. His time was my own. He dared say I would give him a cup of coffee presently.

"I am afraid you will have a poor breakfast," I cried apologetically. "We have been sixty-one days at sea, you know."

A quiet little laugh, with a "That'll be all right, Captain," was his answer. All this, words, intonation, the glimpsed attitude of the man in the cuddy, had an unexpected character, a something friendly in it— propitiatory. And my surprise was not diminished thereby. What did this call mean? Was it the sign of some dark design against my commercial innocence?

Ah! These commercial interests—spoiling the finest life under the sun. Why must the sea be used for trade —and for war as well? Why kill and traffic on it, pursuing selfish aims of no great importance after all? It would have been so much nicer just to sail about with here and there a port and a bit of land to stretch one's legs on, buy a few books and get a change of cooking for a while. But, living in a world more or less homi- cidal and desperately mercantile, it was plainly my duty to make the best of its opportunities.

My owners' letter had left it to me, as I have said before, to do my best for the ship, according to my own judgment. But it contained also a postscript worded somewhat as follows:

"Without meaning to interfere with your liberty of action we are writing by the outgoing mail to some of our business friends there who may be of assistance to you. We desire you particularly to call on Mr. Jacobus, a prominent merchant and charterer. Should you hit it off with him he may be able to put you in the way of profitable employment for the ship."

Hit it off! Here was the prominent creature absolutely on board asking for the favour of a cup of coffee! And life not being a fairy-tale the improbability of the event almost shocked me. Had I discovered an enchanted nook of the earth where wealthy merchants rush fasting on board ships before they are fairly moored? Was this white magic or merely some black trick of trade? I came in the end (while making the bow of my tie) to suspect that perhaps I did not get the name right. I had been thinking of the prominent Mr. Jacobus pretty frequently during the passage and my hearing might have been deceived by some remote similarity of sound. . . . The steward might have said Antrobus—or maybe Jackson.

But coming out of my stateroom with an interrogative "Mr. Jacobus?" I was met by a quiet "Yes," uttered with a gentle smile. The "yes" was rather perfunctory. He did not seem to make much of the fact that he was Mr. Jacobus. I took stock of a big, pale face, hair thin on the top, whiskers also thin, of a faded nondescript colour, heavy eyelids. The thick, smooth lips in repose looked as if glued together. The smile was faint. A heavy, tranquil man. I named my two officers, who just then came down to breakfast; but why Mr. Burns's silent demeanour should suggest suppressed indignation I could not understand.

While we were taking our seats round the table some disconnected words of an altercation going on in the companionway reached my ear. A stranger apparently wanted to come down to interview me, and the steward was opposing him.

"You can't see him."

"Why can't I?"

"The Captain is at breakfast, I tell you. He'll be going on shore presently, and you can speak to him on deck."

"That's not fair. You let——"

"I've had nothing to do with that."

"Oh, yes, you have. Everybody ought to have the same chance. You let that fellow——"

The rest I lost. The person having been repulsed successfully, the steward came down. I can't say he looked flushed—he was a mulatto—but he looked flustered. After putting the dishes on the table he remained by the sideboard with that lackadaisical air of indifference he used to assume when he had done something too clever by half and was afraid of getting into a scrape over it. The contemptuous expression of Mr. Burns's face as he looked from him to me was really extraordinary. I couldn't imagine what new bee had stung the mate now.

The Captain being silent, nobody else cared to speak, as is the way in ships. And I was saying nothing simply because I had been made dumb by the splendour of the entertainment. I had expected the usual sea-breakfast, whereas I beheld spread before us a veritable feast of shore provisions: eggs, sausages, butter which plainly did not come from a Danish tin, cutlets, and even a dish of potatoes. It was three weeks since I had seen a real, live potato. I contemplated them with interest, and Mr. Jacobus disclosed himself as a man of human, homely sympathies, and something of a thought-reader.

"Try them, Captain," he encouraged me in a friendly undertone. "They are excellent."

"They look that," I admitted. "Grown on the island, I suppose."

"Oh, no, imported. Those grown here would be more expensive."

I was grieved at the ineptitude of the conversation. Were these the topics for a prominent and wealthy merchant to discuss? I thought the simplicity with which he made himself at home rather attractive; but what is one to talk about to a man who comes on one suddenly, after sixty-one days at sea, out of a totally unknown little town in an island one has never seen before? What were (besides sugar) the interests of that crumb of the earth, its gossip, its topics of conversation? To draw him on business at once would have been almost indecent—or even worse: impolitic. All I could do at the moment was to keep on in the old groove.

"Are the provisions generally dear here?" I asked, fretting inwardly at my inanity.

"I wouldn't say that," he answered placidly, with that appearance of saving his breath his restrained manner of speaking suggested.

He would not be more explicit, yet he did not evade the subject. Eyeing the table in a spirit of complete abstemiousness (he wouldn't let me help him to any eatables) he went into details of supply. The beef was for the most part imported from Madagascar; mutton of course was rare and somewhat expensive, but good goat's flesh——

"Are these goat's cutlets?" I exclaimed hastily, pointing at one of the dishes.

Posed sentimentally by the sideboard, the steward gave a start.

"Lor', no, sir! It's real mutton!"

Mr. Burns got through his breakfast impatiently, as if exasperated by being made a party to some monstrous foolishness, muttered a curt excuse, and went on deck. Shortly afterwards the second mate took his smooth red countenance out of the cabin. With the appetite of a schoolboy, and after two months of sea-fare, he appreciated the generous spread. But I did not. It smacked of extravagance. All the same, it was a remarkable feat to have produced it so quickly, and I congratulated the steward on his smartness in a somewhat ominous tone. He gave me a deprecatory smile and, in a way I didn't know what to make of, blinked his fine dark eyes in the direction of the guest.

The latter asked under his breath for another cup of coffee, and nibbled ascetically at a piece of very hard ship's biscuit. I don't think he consumed a square inch in the end; but meantime he gave me, casually as it were, a complete account of the sugar crop, of the local business houses, of the state of the freight market. All that talk was interspersed with hints as to personalities, amounting to veiled warnings, but his pale, fleshy face remained equable, without a gleam, as if ignorant of his voice. As you may imagine I opened my ears very wide. Every word was precious. My ideas as to the value of business friendship were being favourably modified. He gave me the names of all the disponible ships together with their tonnage and the names of their commanders. From that, which was still commercial information, he condescended to mere harbour gossip. The *Hilda* had unaccountably lost her figure-head in the Bay of Bengal, and her captain was greatly affected by this. He and the ship had been getting on in years together and the old gentleman imagined this strange event to be the fore-runner of his own early dissolution. The *Stella* had experienced awful weather off the Cape—had her decks swept, and the chief officer washed overboard. And only a few hours before reaching port the baby died. Poor Captain H—— and his wife were terribly cut up. If they had only been able to bring it into port alive it could have been probably saved; but the wind failed them for the last week or so, light breezes, and . . . the baby was going to be buried this afternoon. He supposed I would attend——

"Do you think I ought to?" I asked, shrinkingly.

He thought so, decidedly. It would be greatly appreciated. All the captains in the harbour were going to attend. Poor Mrs. H—— was quite prostrated. Pretty hard on H—— altogether.

"And you, Captain—you are not married I suppose?"

"No, I am not married," I said. "Neither married nor even engaged."

Mentally I thanked my stars; and while he smiled in a musing, dreamy fashion, I expressed my acknowledgments for his visit and for the interesting business information he had been good enough to impart to me. But I said nothing of my wonder thereat.

"Of course, I would have made a point of calling on you in a day or two," I concluded.

He raised his eyelids distinctly at me, and somehow managed to look rather more sleepy than before.

"In accordance with my owners' instructions," I explained. "You have had their letter, of course?"

By that time he had raised his eyebrows too but without any particular emotion. On the contrary he struck me then as absolutely imperturbable.

"Oh! You must be thinking of my brother."

It was for me, then, to say "Oh!" But I hope that
no more than civil surprise appeared in my voice when
I asked him to what, then, I owed the pleasure. . . .
He was reaching for an inside pocket leisurely.

"My brother's a very different person. But I am
well known in this part of the world. You've probably
heard——"

I took a card he extended to me. A thick business
card, as I lived! Alfred Jacobus—the other was
Ernest—dealer in every description of ship's stores!
Provisions salt and fresh, oils, paints, rope, canvas,
etc., etc. Ships in harbour victualled by contract on
moderate terms——

"I've never heard of you," I said brusquely.

His low-pitched assurance did not abandon him.

"You will be very well satisfied," he breathed out
quietly.

I was not placated. I had the sense of having been
circumvented somehow. Yet I had deceived myself
—if there was any deception. But the confounded
cheek of inviting himself to breakfast was enough to
deceive any one. And the thought struck me: Why!
The fellow had provided all these eatables himself in
the way of business. I said:

"You must have got up mighty early this morning."

He admitted with simplicity that he was on the quay
before six o'clock waiting for my ship to come in. He
gave me the impression that it would be impossible to
get rid of him now.

"If you think we are going to live on that scale," I
said, looking at the table with an irritated eye, "you
are jolly well mistaken."

"You'll find it all right, Captain. I quite understand."

Nothing could disturb his equanimity. I felt dis.

satisfied, but I could not very well fly out at him. He had told me many useful things—and besides he was the brother of that wealthy merchant. That seemed queer enough.

I rose and told him curtly that I must now go ashore. At once he offered the use of his boat for all the time of my stay in port.

"I only make a nominal charge," he continued equably. "My man remains all day at the landing-steps. You have only to blow a whistle when you want the boat."

And, standing aside at every doorway to let me go through first, he carried me off in his custody after all. As we crossed the quarter-deck two shabby individuals stepped forward and in mournful silence offered me business cards which I took from them without a word under his heavy eye. It was a useless and gloomy ceremony. They were the touts of the other ship-chandlers, and he, placid at my back, ignored their existence.

We parted on the quay, after he had expressed quietly the hope of seeing me often "at the store." He had a smoking-room for captains there, with news-papers and a box of "rather decent cigars." I left him very unceremoniously.

My consignees received me with the usual business heartiness, but their account of the state of the freight-market was by no means so favourable as the talk of the wrong Jacobus had led me to expect. Naturally I became inclined now to put my trust in his version, rather. As I closed the door of the private office behind me I thought to myself: "H'm. A lot of lies. Commercial diplomacy. That's the sort of thing a man coming from sea has got to expect. They would try to charter the ship under the market rate."

In the big, outer room, full of desks, the chief clerk, a tall, lean, shaved person in immaculate white clothes and with a shiny, closely cropped black head on which silvery gleams came and went, rose from his place and detained me affably. Anything they could do for me, they would be most happy. Was I likely to call again in the afternoon? What? Going to a funeral? Oh, yes, poor Captain H——.

He pulled a long, sympathetic face for a moment, then, dismissing from this workaday world the baby, which had got ill in a tempest and had died from too much calm at sea, he asked me with a dental, shark-like smile—if sharks had false teeth—whether I had yet made my little arrangements for the ship's stay in port.

"Yes, with Jacobus," I answered carelessly. "I understand he's the brother of Mr. Ernest Jacobus to whom I have an introduction from my owners."

I was not sorry to let him know I was not altogether helpless in the hands of his firm. He screwed his thin lips dubiously.

"Why," I cried, "isn't he the brother?"

"Oh, yes. . . . They haven't spoken to each other for eighteen years," he added impressively after a pause.

"Indeed! What's the quarrel about?"

"Oh, nothing! Nothing that one would care to mention," he protested primly. "He's got quite a large business. The best ship-chandler here, without a doubt. Business is all very well, but there is such a thing as personal character, too, isn't there? Good-morning, Captain."

He went away mincingly to his desk. He amused me. He resembled an old maid, a commercial old maid, shocked by some impropriety. Was it a commercial impropriety? Commercial impropriety is a serious matter, for it aims at one's pocket. Or was he only a purist in conduct who disapproved of Jacobus doing his own touting? It was certainly undignified. I wondered how the merchant brother liked it. But then different countries, different customs. In a community so isolated and so exclusively "trading" social standards have their own scale.

II

I WOULD have gladly dispensed with the mournful opportunity of becoming acquainted by sight with all my fellow-captains at once. However I found my way to the cemetery. We made a considerable group of bareheaded men in sombre garments. I noticed that those of our company most approaching to the now obsolete sea-dog type were the most moved—perhaps because they had less "manner" than the new generation. The old sea-dog, away from his natural element, was a simple and sentimental animal. I noticed one—he was facing me across the grave—who was dropping tears. They trickled down his weather-beaten face like drops of rain on an old rugged wall. I learned afterwards that he was looked upon as the terror of sailors, a hard man; that he had never had wife or chick of his own, and that, engaged from his tenderest years in deep-sea voyages, he knew women and children merely by sight.

Perhaps he was dropping those tears over his lost opportunities, from sheer envy of paternity and in strange jealousy of a sorrow which he could never know. Man, and even the sea-man, is a capricious animal, the creature and the victim of lost opportunities. But he made me feel ashamed of my callousness. I had no tears.

I listened with horribly critical detachment to that service I had had to read myself, once or twice, over childlike men who had died at sea. The words of hope and defiance, the winged words so inspiring in the free immensity of water and sky, seemed to fall wearily into the little grave. What was the use of asking Death where her sting was, before that small, dark hole in the ground? And then my thoughts escaped me altogether —away into matters of life—and no very high matters at that—ships, freights, business. In the instability of his emotions man resembles deplorably a monkey. I was disgusted with my thoughts—and I thought: Shall I be able to get a charter soon? Time's money. . . Will that Jacobus really put good business in my way? . . . I must go and see him in a day or two.

Don't imagine that I pursued these thoughts with any precision. They pursued me rather: vague, shadowy, restless, shamefaced. Theirs was a callous, abominable, almost revolting, pertinacity. And it was the presence of that pertinacious ship-chandler which had started them. He stood mournfully amongst our little band of men from the sea, and I was angry at his presence, which, suggesting his brother the merchant, had caused me to become outrageous to myself. For indeed I had preserved some decency of feeling. It was only the mind which——

It was over at last. The poor father—a man of forty with black, bushy side-whiskers and a pathetic gash on his freshly shaved chin—thanked us all, swallowing his tears. But for some reason, either because I lingered at the gate of the cemetery, being somewhat hazy as to my way back, or because I was the youngest, or ascribing my moodiness caused by remorse to some more worthy and appropriate sentiment, or simply because I was even more of a stranger to him than the others—he singled me out. Keeping at my side, he renewed his thanks, which I listened to in a gloomy, conscience-stricken silence. Suddenly he slipped one hand under my arm and waved the other after a tall, stout figure walking away by itself down a street in a flutter of thin, grey garments:

"That's a good fellow—a real good fellow"—he swallowed down a belated sob—"this Jacobus."

And he told me in a low voice that Jacobus was the first man to board his ship on arrival, and, learning of their misfortune, had taken charge of everything, volunteered to attend to all routine business, carried off the ship's papers on shore, arranged for the funeral——

"A good fellow. I was knocked over. I had been looking at my wife for ten days. And helpless. Just you think of that! The dear little chap died the very day we made the land. How I managed to take the ship in God alone knows! I couldn't see anything; I couldn't speak; I couldn't. . . . You've heard, perhaps, that we lost our mate overboard on the passage? There was no one to do it for me. And the poor woman nearly crazy down below there all alone with the . . . By the Lord! It isn't fair."

We walked in silence together. I did not know how to part from him. On the quay he let go my arm and struck fiercely his fist into the palm of his other hand.

"By God, it isn't fair!" he cried again. "Don't you ever marry unless you can chuck the sea first. . . . It isn't fair."

I had no intention to "chuck the sea," and when he left me to go aboard his ship I felt convinced that I would never marry. While I was waiting at the steps for Jacobus's boatman, who had gone off somewhere, the captain of the *Hilda* joined me, a slender silk umbrella in his hand and the sharp points of his archaic,

Gladstonian shirt-collar framing a small, clean-shaved ruddy face.   It was wonderfully fresh for his age, beautifully modelled and lit up by remarkably clear blue eyes.   A lot of white hair, glossy like spun glass, curled upwards slightly under the brim of his valuable, ancient, panama hat with a broad black ribbon.   In the aspect of that vivacious, neat, little old man there was something quaintly angelic and also boyish.

He accosted me, as though he had been in the habit of seeing me every day of his life from my earliest child-hood, with a whimsical remark on the appearance of a stout negro woman who was sitting upon a stool near the edge of the quay.   Presently he observed amiably that I had a very pretty little barque.

I returned this civil speech by saying readily:

"Not so pretty as the *Hilda*."

At once the corners of his clear-cut, sensitive mouth dropped dismally.

"Oh, dear!   I can hardly bear to look at her now."

Did I know, he asked anxiously, that he had lost the figurehead of his ship; a woman in a blue tunic edged with gold, the face perhaps not so very, very pretty, but her bare white arms beautifully shaped and extended as if she were swimming? Did I?   Who would have expected such a thing! . . . After twenty years too!

Nobody could have guessed from his tone that the woman was made of wood; his trembling voice, his agitated manner gave to his lamentations a ludicrously scandalous flavour. . . .   Disappeared at night— a clear fine night with just a slight swell—in the gulf of Bengal.   Went off without a splash; no one in the ship could tell why, how, at what hour—after twenty years last October. . . . Did I ever hear. . . .

I assured him sympathetically that I had never heard

—and he became very doleful. This meant no good he was sure. There was something in it which looked like a warning. But when I remarked that surely another figure of a woman could be procured I found myself being soundly rated for my levity. The old boy flushed pink under his clear tan as if I had proposed something improper. One could replace masts, I was told, or a lost rudder—any working part of a ship; but where was the use of sticking up a new figurehead? What satisfaction? How could one care for it? It was easy to see that I had never been shipmates with a figurehead for over twenty years.

"A new figurehead!" he scolded in unquenchable indignation. "Why! I've been a widower now for eight-and-twenty years come next May and I would just as soon think of getting a new wife. You're as bad as that fellow Jacobus."

I was highly amused.

"What has Jacobus done? Did he want you to marry again, Captain?" I inquired in a deferential tone. But he was launched now and only grinned fiercely.

"Procure—indeed! He's the sort of chap to procure you anything you like for a price. I hadn't been moored here for an hour when he got on board and at once offered to sell me a figurehead he happens to have in his yard somewhere. He got Smith, my mate, to talk to me about it. 'Mr. Smith,' says I, 'don't you know me better than that? Am I the sort that would pick up with another man's cast-off figurehead?' And after all these years too! The way some of you young fellows talk——"

I affected great compunction, and as I stepped into the boat I said soberly:

"Then I see nothing for it but to fit in a neat fiddle-head—perhaps. You know, carved scrollwork, nicely gilt."

He became very dejected after his outburst.

"Yes. Scrollwork. Maybe. Jacobus hinted at that too. He's never at a loss when there's any money to be extracted from a sailorman. He would make me pay through the nose for that carving. A gilt fiddle-head did you say—eh? I dare say it would do for you. You young fellows don't seem to have any feeling for what's proper."

He made a convulsive gesture with his right arm.

"Never mind. Nothing can make much difference. I would just as soon let the old thing go about the world with a bare cutwater," he cried sadly. Then as the boat got away from the steps he raised his voice on the edge of the quay with comical animosity:

"I would! If only to spite that figurehead-procuring bloodsucker. I am an old bird here and don't you forget it. Come and see me on board some day!"

I spent my first evening in port quietly in my ship's cuddy; and glad enough was I to think that the shore life which strikes one as so pettily complex, discordant, and so full of new faces on first coming from sea, could be kept off for a few hours longer. I was however fated to hear the Jacobus note once more before I slept.

Mr. Burns had gone ashore after the evening meal to have, as he said, "a look round." As it was quite dark when he announced his intention I didn't ask him what it was he expected to see. Some time about midnight, while sitting with a book in the saloon, I heard cautious movements in the lobby and hailed him by name.

Burns came in, stick and hat in hand, incredibly vulgarised by his smart shore togs, with a jaunty air and an odious twinkle in his eye. Being asked to sit down he laid his hat and stick on the table and after we had talked of ship affairs for a little while:

"I've been hearing pretty tales on shore about that ship-chandler fellow who snatched the job from you so neatly, sir."

I remonstrated with my late patient for his manner of expressing himself. But he only tossed his head disdainfully. A pretty dodge indeed: boarding a strange ship with breakfast in two baskets for all hands and calmly inviting himself to the captain's table! Never heard of anything so crafty and so impudent in his life.

I found myself defending Jacobus's unusual methods.

"He's the brother of one of the wealthiest merchants in the port." The mate's eyes fairly snapped green sparks.

"His grand brother hasn't spoken to him for eighteen or twenty years," he declared triumphantly. "So there!"

"I know all about that," I interrupted loftily.

"Do you, sir? H'm!" His mind was still running on the ethics of commercial competition. "I don't like to see your good nature taken advantage of. He's bribed that steward of ours with a five-rupee note to let him come down—or ten for that matter. He don't care. He will shove that and more into the bill presently."

"Is that one of the tales you have heard ashore?" I asked.

He assured me that his own sense could tell him that much. No; what he had heard on shore was that no respectable person in the whole town would come near Jacobus. He lived in a large old-fashioned house in one of the quiet streets with a big garden. After telling me this Burns put on a mysterious air. "He keeps a girl shut up there who, they say——"

"I suppose you've heard all this gossip in some eminently respectable place?" I snapped at him in a most sarcastic tone.

The shaft told, because Mr. Burns, like many other disagreeable people, was very sensitive himself. He remained as if thunderstruck, with his mouth open for some further communication, but I did not give him the chance. "And, anyhow, what the deuce do I care?" I added, retiring into my room.

And this was a natural thing to say. Yet somehow I was not indifferent. I admit it is absurd to be concerned with the morals of one's ship-chandler, if ever so well connected; but his personality had stamped itself upon my first day in harbour, in the way you know.

After this initial exploit Jacobus showed himself anything but intrusive. He was out in a boat early every morning going round the ships he served, and occasionally remaining on board one of them for breakfast with the captain.

As I discovered that this practice was generally accepted, I just nodded to him familiarly when one morning, on coming out of my room, I found him in the cabin. Glancing over the table I saw that his place was already laid. He stood awaiting my appearance, very bulky and placid, holding a beautiful bunch of flowers in his thick hand. He offered them to my notice with a faint, sleepy smile. From his own garden; had a very fine old garden; picked them himself that morning before going out to business; thought I would like. . . . He turned away. "Steward, can you oblige me with some water in a large jar, please?"

I assured him jocularly, as I took my place at the table, that he made me feel as if I were a pretty girl, and that he mustn't be surprised if I blushed. But he was busy arranging his floral tribute at the sideboard. "Stand it before the Captain's plate, steward, please." He made his request in his usual undertone.

The offering was so pointed that I could do no less than to raise it to my nose, and as he sat down noiselessly he breathed out the opinion that a few flowers improved notably the appearance of a ship's saloon. He wondered why I did not have a shelf fitted all round the skylight for flowers in pots to take with me to sea. He had a skilled workman able to fit up shelves in a day, and he could procure me two or three dozen good plants——

The tips of his thick, round fingers rested composedly on the edge of the table on each side of his cup of coffee. His face remained immovable. Mr. Burns was smiling maliciously to himself. I declared that I hadn't the slightest intention of turning my skylight into a conservatory only to keep the cabin-table in a perpetual mess of mould and dead vegetable matter.

"Rear most beautiful flowers," he insisted with an upward glance. "It's no trouble really."

"Oh, yes, it is. Lots of trouble," I contradicted. "And in the end some fool leaves the skylight open in a fresh breeze, a flick of salt water gets at them and the whole lot is dead in a week."

Mr. Burns snorted a contemptuous approval. Jacobus gave up the subject passively. After a time he unglued his thick lips to ask me if I had seen his brother yet. I was very curt in my answer.

"No, not yet."

"A very different person," he remarked dreamily and got up. His movements were particularly noiseless. "Well—thank you, Captain. If anything is not to your liking please mention it to your steward. I suppose you will be giving a dinner to the office-clerks presently."

"What for?" I cried with some warmth. "If I were a steady trader to the port I could understand it. But a complete stranger! . . . I may not turn up again here for years. I don't see why I . . . Do you mean to say it is customary?"

"It will be expected from a man like you," he breathed out placidly. "Eight of the principal clerks, the manager, that's nine, you three gentlemen, that's twelve. It needn't be very expensive. If you tell your steward to give me a day's notice——"

"It will be expected of me! Why should it be expected of me? Is it because I look particularly soft— or what?"

His immobility struck me as dignified suddenly, his imperturbable quality as dangerous. "There's plenty of time to think about that," I concluded weakly with a gesture that tried to wave him away. But before he departed he took time to mention regretfully that he had not yet had the pleasure of seeing me at his "store" to sample those cigars. He had a parcel of six thousand to dispose of, very cheap.

"I think it would be worth your while to secure some," he added with a fat, melancholy smile and left the cabin.

Mr. Burns struck his fist on the table excitedly.

"Did you ever see such impudence! He's made up his mind to get something out of you one way or another, sir."

At once feeling inclined to defend Jacobus, I observed philosophically that all this was business, I supposed. But my absurd mate, muttering broken disjointed sentences, such as: "I cannot bear! . . . Mark my words! . . ." and so on, flung out of the cabin.

If I hadn't nursed him through that deadly fever I wouldn't have suffered such manners for a single day.

III

JACOBUS having put me in mind of his wealthy brother I concluded I would pay that business call at once. I had by that time heard a little more of him. He was a member of the Council, where he made himself objectionable to the authorities. He exercised a considerable influence on public opinion. Lots of people owed him money. He was an importer on a great scale of all sorts of goods. For instance, the whole supply of bags for sugar was practically in his hands. This last fact I did not learn till afterwards. The general impression conveyed to me was that of a local personage. He was a bachelor and gave weekly card-parties in his house out of town, which were attended by the best people in the colony.

The greater, then, was my surprise to discover his office in shabby surroundings, quite away from the business quarter, amongst a lot of hovels. Guided by a black board with white lettering, I climbed a narrow wooden staircase and entered a room with a bare floor of planks littered with bits of brown paper and wisps of packing straw. A great number of what looked like wine-cases were piled up against one of the walls. A lanky, inky, light-yellow, mulatto youth, miserably long-necked and generally recalling a sick chicken, got off a three-legged stool behind a cheap deal desk and faced me as if gone dumb with fright. I had some difficulty in persuading him to take in my name, though I could not get from him the nature of his objection. He did it at last with an almost agonised reluctance which ceased to be mysterious to me when I heard him being sworn at menacingly with savage, suppressed growls, then audibly cuffed and finally kicked out without any concealment whatever; because he came back flying head foremost through the door with a stifled shriek.

To say I was startled would not express it. I remained still, like a man lost in a dream. Clapping both his hands to that part of his frail anatomy which had received the shock, the poor wretch said to me simply: "Will you go in, please."

His lamentable self-possession was wonderful; but it did not do away with the incredibility of the experience. A preposterous notion that I had seen this boy somewhere before, a thing obviously impossible, was like a delicate finishing touch of weirdness added to a scene fit to raise doubts as to one's sanity. I stared anxiously about me like an awakened somnambulist.

"I say," I cried loudly, "there isn't a mistake, is there? This is Mr. Jacobus's office?"

The boy gazed at me with a pained expression—and somehow so familiar! A voice within growled offensively:

"Come in, come in, since you are there. . . . I didn't know."

I crossed the outer room as one approaches the den of some unknown wild beast; with intrepidity but in some excitement. Only no wild beast that ever lived would rouse one's indignation; the power to do that belongs to the odiousness of the human brute. And I was very indignant, which did not prevent me from being at once struck by the extraordinary resemblance of the two brothers.

This one was dark instead of being fair like the other; but he was as big. He was without his coat and waistcoat; he had been doubtless snoozing in the rocking-chair which stood in a corner furthest from the window. Above the great bulk of his crumpled white shirt, buttoned with three diamond studs, his round face looked swarthy. It was moist; his brown moustache hung limp and ragged. He pushed a common, cane-bottomed chair towards me with his foot.

"Sit down."

I glanced at it casually, then, turning my indignant eyes full upon him, I declared in precise and incisive tones that I had called in obedience to my owners' instructions.

"Oh! Yes. H'm! I didn't understand what that fool was saying. . . . But never mind! It will teach the scoundrel to disturb me at this time of the day," he added, grinning at me with savage cynicism.

I looked at my watch. It was past three o'clock— quite the full swing of afternoon office work in the port. He snarled imperiously: "Sit down, Captain."

I acknowledged the gracious invitation by saying deliberately:

"I can listen to all you may have to say without sitting down."

Emitting a loud and vehement "Pshaw!" he glared for a moment, very round-eyed and fierce. It was like a gigantic tomcat spitting at one suddenly. "Look at him! . . . What do you fancy yourself to be? What did you come here for? If you won't sit down and talk business you had better go to the devil."

"I don't know him personally," I said. "But after this I wouldn't mind calling on him. It would be refreshing to meet a gentleman."

He followed me, growling behind my back:

"The impudence! I've a good mind to write to your owners what I think of you."

I turned on him for a moment:

"As it happens I don't care. For my part I assure you I won't even take the trouble to mention you to them."

He stopped at the door of his office while I traversed the littered anteroom. I think he was somewhat taken aback.

"I will break every bone in your body," he roared suddenly at the miserable mulatto lad, "if you ever dare to disturb me before half-past three for anybody. D'ye hear? For anybody! . . . Let alone any damned skipper," he added, in a lower growl.

The frail youngster, swaying like a reed, made a low moaning sound. I stopped short and addressed this sufferer with advice. It was prompted by the sight of a hammer (used for opening the wine-cases, I suppose) which was lying on the floor.

"If I were you, my boy, I would have that thing up my sleeve when I went in next and at the first occasion I would——"

What was there so familiar in that lad's yellow face? Entrenched and quaking behind the flimsy desk, he never looked up. His heavy, lowered eyelids gave me suddenly the clue of the puzzle. He resembled—yes, those thick glued lips—he resembled the brothers Jacobus. He resembled both, the wealthy merchant and the pushing shopkeeper (who resembled each other); he resembled them as much as a thin, light-yellow mulatto lad may resemble a big, stout, middle-aged white man. It was the exotic complexion and the slightness of his build which had put me off so completely. Now I saw in him unmistakably the Jacobus strain, weakened, attenuated, diluted as it were in a bucket of water—and I refrained from finishing my speech. I had intended to say: "Crack this brute's head for him." I still felt the conclusion to be sound. But it is no trifling responsibility to counsel parricide to any one, however deeply injured.

"Beggarly—cheeky—skippers."

I despised the emphatic growl at my back; only, being much vexed and upset, I regret to say that I slammed the door behind me in a most undignified manner.

It may not appear altogether absurd if I say that I brought out from that interview a kindlier view of the other Jacobus. It was with a feeling resembling partisanship that, a few days later, I called at his "store." That long, cavern-like place of business, very dim at the back and stuffed full of all sorts of goods, was entered from the street by a lofty archway. At the far end I saw my Jacobus exerting himself in his shirt-sleeves among his assistants. The captains' room was a small, vaulted apartment with a stone floor and heavy iron bars in its windows like a dungeon converted to hospitable purposes. A couple of cheerful bottles and several gleaming glasses made a brilliant cluster round a tall, cool red earthenware pitcher on the centre table which was littered with newspapers from all parts of the world. A well-groomed stranger in a smart grey check suit, sitting with one leg flung over his knee, put down one of these sheets briskly and nodded to me.

I guessed him to be a steamer-captain. It was impossible to get to know these men. They came and went too quickly and their ships lay moored far out, at the very entrance of the harbour. Theirs was another life altogether. He yawned slightly.

"Dull hole, isn't it?"

I understood this to allude to the town.

"Do you find it so?" I murmured.

"Don't you? But I'm off to-morrow, thank goodness."

He was a very gentlemanly person, good-natured and superior. I watched him draw the open box of cigars to his side of the table, take a big cigar-case out of his pocket and begin to fill it very methodically. Presently, on our eyes meeting, he winked like a common mortal and invited me to follow his example. "They are really decent smokes." I shook my head.

"I am not off to-morrow."

"What of that? Think I am abusing old Jacobus's hospitality? Heavens! It goes into the bill, of course. He spreads such little matters all over his account. He can take care of himself! Why, it's business——"

I noted a shadow fall over his well-satisfied expression, a momentary hesitation in closing his cigar-case. But he ended by putting it in his pocket jauntily. A placid voice uttered in the doorway: "That's quite correct, Captain."

The large noiseless Jacobus advanced into the room. His quietness, in the circumstances, amounted to cordiality. He had put on his jacket before joining us, and he sat down in the chair vacated by the steamer-man, who nodded again to me and went out with a short, jarring laugh. A profound silence reigned. With his drowsy stare Jacobus seemed to be slumbering open-eyed. Yet, somehow, I was aware of being profoundly scrutinised by those heavy eyes. In the enormous cavern of the store somebody began to nail down a case, expertly: tap-tap . . . tap-tap-tap. Two other experts, one slow and nasal, the other shrill and snappy, started checking an invoice.

"A half-coil of three-inch manilla rope."

"Right!"

"Six assorted shackles."

"Right!"

"Six tins assorted soups, three of paté, two asparagus, fourteen pounds tobacco, cabin."

"Right!"

"It's for the captain who was here just now," breathed out the immovable Jacobus. "These steamer orders are very small. They pick up what they want as they go along. That man will be in Samarang in less than a fortnight. Very small orders indeed."

The calling over of the items went on in the shop; an extraordinary jumble of varied articles, paint-brushes, Yorkshire Relish, etc., etc. . . . "Three sacks of best potatoes," read out the nasal voice.

At this Jacobus blinked like a sleeping man roused by a shake, and displayed some animation. At his order, shouted into the shop, a smirking half-caste clerk with his ringlets much oiled and with a pen stuck behind his ear, brought in a sample of six potatoes which he paraded in a row on the table.

Being urged to look at their beauty I gave them a cold and hostile glance. Calmly, Jacobus proposed that I should order ten or fifteen tons—tons! I couldn't believe my ears. My crew could not have eaten such a lot in a year; and potatoes (excuse these practical remarks) are a highly perishable commodity. I thought he was joking—or else trying to find out whether I was an unutterable idiot. But his purpose was not so simple. I discovered that he meant me to buy them on my own account.

"I am proposing you a bit of business, Captain. I wouldn't charge you a great price."

I told him that I did not go in for trade. I even

added grimly that I knew only too well how that sort of spec. generally ended.

He sighed and clasped his hands on his stomach with exemplary resignation. I admired the placidity of his impudence. Then waking up somewhat:

"Won't you try a cigar, Captain?"

"No, thanks. I don't smoke cigars."

"For once!" he exclaimed, in a patient whisper. A melancholy silence ensued. You know how sometimes a person discloses a certain unsuspected depth and acuteness of thought; that is, in other words, utters something unexpected. It was unexpected enough to hear Jacobus say:

"The man who just went out was right enough. You might take one, Captain. Here everything is bound to be in the way of business."

I felt a little ashamed of myself. The remembrance of his horrid brother made him appear quite a decent sort of fellow. It was with some compunction that I said a few words to the effect that I could have no possible objection to his hospitality.

Before I was a minute older I saw where this admission was leading me. As if changing the subject Jacobus mentioned that his private house was about ten minutes' walk away. It had a beautiful old walled garden. Something really remarkable. I ought to come round some day and have a look at it.

He seemed to be a lover of gardens. I too take extreme delight in them; but I did not mean my compunction to carry me as far as Jacobus's flower-beds, however beautiful and old. He added, with a certain homeliness of tone:

"There's only my girl there."

It is difficult to set everything down in due order; so I must revert here to what happened a week or two before. The medical officer of the port had come on board my ship to have a look at one of my crew who was ailing, and naturally enough he was asked to step into the cabin. A fellow-shipmaster of mine was there too; and in the conversation, somehow or other, the name of Jacobus came to be mentioned. It was pronounced with no particular reverence by the other man, I believe. I don't remember now what I was going to say. The doctor—a pleasant, cultivated fellow, with an assured manner—prevented me by striking in, in a sour tone:

"Ah! You're talking about my respected papa-in-law."

Of course, that sally silenced us at the time. But I remembered the episode, and at this juncture, pushed for something non-committal to say, I inquired with polite surprise:

"You have your married daughter living with you, Mr. Jacobus?"

He moved his big hand from right to left quietly. No! That was another of his girls, he stated, ponderously and under his breath as usual. She . . . He seemed in a pause to be ransacking his mind for some kind of descriptive phrase. But my hopes were disappointed. He merely produced his stereotyped definition.

"She's a very different sort of person."

"Indeed. . . . And by the by, Jacobus, I called on your brother the other day. It's no great compliment if I say that I found him a very different sort of person from you."

He had an air of profound reflection, then remarked quaintly:

"He's a man of regular habits."

He might have been alluding to the habit of late

siesta; but I mumbled something about "beastly habits anyhow"—and left the store abruptly.

IV

My little passage with Jacobus the merchant became known generally. One or two of my acquaintances made distant allusions to it. Perhaps the mulatto boy had talked. I must confess that people appeared rather scandalised, but not with Jacobus's brutality. A man I knew remonstrated with me for my hastiness.

I gave him the whole story of my visit, not forgetting the tell-tale resemblance of the wretched mulatto boy to his tormentor. He was not surprised. No doubt, no doubt. What of that? In a jovial tone he assured me that there must be many of that sort. The elder Jacobus had been a bachelor all his life. A highly respectable bachelor. But there had never been open scandal in that connection. His life had been quite regular. It could cause no offence to any one.

I said that I had been offended considerably. My interlocutor opened very wide eyes. Why? Because a mulatto lad got a few knocks? That was not a great affair, surely. I had no idea how insolent and untruthful these half-castes were. In fact he seemed to think Mr. Jacobus rather kind than otherwise to employ that youth at all; a sort of amiable weakness which could be forgiven.

This acquaintance of mine belonged to one of the old French families, descendants of the old colonists; all noble, all impoverished, and living a narrow domestic life in dull, dignified decay. The men, as a rule, occupy inferior posts in Government offices or in business houses. The girls are almost always pretty, ignorant of the world, kind and agreeable and generally bilingual;

they prattle innocently both in French and English.
The emptiness of their existence passes belief.

I obtained my entry into a couple of such house-
holds because some years before, in Bombay, I had
occasion to be of use to a pleasant, ineffectual young
man who was rather stranded there, not knowing what
to do with himself or even how to get home to his island
again. It was a matter of two hundred rupees or so,
but, when I turned up, the family made a point of showing their gratitude by admitting me to their intimacy.
My knowledge of the French language made me
specially acceptable. They had meantime managed to
marry the fellow to a woman nearly twice his age,
comparatively well off: the only profession he was really
fit for. But it was not all cakes and ale. The first
time I called on the couple she spied a little spot of
grease on the poor devil's pantaloons and made him a
screaming scene of reproaches so full of sincere passion
that I sat terrified as at a tragedy of Racine.

Of course there was never question of the money I
had advanced him; but his sisters, Miss Angele and
Miss Mary, and the aunts of both families, who spoke
quaint archaic French of pre-Revolution period, and
a host of distant relations adopted me for a friend outright in a manner which was almost embarrassing.

It was with the eldest brother (he was employed at
a desk in my consignee's office) that I was having this
talk about the merchant Jacobus. He regretted my
attitude and nodded his head sagely. An influential
man. One never knew when one would need him. I
expressed my immense preference for the shopkeeper
of the two. At that my friend looked grave.

"What on earth are you pulling that long face
about?" I cried impatiently. "He asked me to see
his garden and I have a good mind to go some day."

"Don't do that," he said, so earnestly that I burst into a fit of laughter; but he looked at me without a smile.

This was another matter altogether. At one time the public conscience of the island had been mightily troubled by my Jacobus. The two brothers had been partners for years in great harmony, when a wandering circus came to the island and my Jacobus became suddenly infatuated with one of the lady-riders. What made it worse was that he was married. He had not even the grace to conceal his passion. It must have been strong indeed to carry away such a large placid creature. His behaviour was perfectly scandalous.

He followed that woman to the Cape, and apparently travelled at the tail of that beastly circus to other parts of the world, in a most degrading position. The woman soon ceased to care for him, and treated him worse than a dog. Most extraordinary stories of moral degradation were reaching the island at that time. He had not the strength of mind to shake himself free. . . .

The grotesque image of a fat, pushing ship-chandler, enslaved by an unholy love-spell, fascinated me; and I listened rather open-mouthed to the tale as old as the world, a tale which had been the subject of legend, of moral fables, of poems, but which so ludicrously failed to fit the personality. What a strange victim for the gods!

Meantime his deserted wife had died. His daughter was taken care of by his brother, who married her as advantageously as was possible in the circumstances.

"Oh! The Mrs. Doctor!" I exclaimed.

"You know that? Yes. A very able man. He wanted a lift in the world, and there was a good bit of money from her mother, besides the expectations. . . . Of course, they don't know him," he added.

"The doctor nods in the street, I believe, but he avoids speaking to him when they meet on board a ship, as must happen sometimes."

I remarked that this surely was an old story by now.

My friend assented. But it was Jacobus's own fault that it was neither forgiven nor forgotten. He came back ultimately. But how? Not in a spirit of contrition, in a way to propitiate his scandalised fellow-citizens. He must needs drag along with him a child—a girl. . . .

"He spoke to me of a daughter who lives with him," I observed, very much interested.

"She's certainly the daughter of the circus-woman," said my friend. "She may be his daughter too; I am willing to admit that she is. In fact I have no doubt——"

But he did not see why she should have been brought into a respectable community to perpetuate the memory of the scandal. And that was not the worst. Presently something much more distressing happened. That abandoned woman turned up. Landed from a mail-boat. . . .

"What! Here? To claim the child perhaps," I suggested.

"Not she!" My friendly informant was very scornful. "Imagine a painted, haggard, agitated, desperate hag. Been cast off in Mozambique by somebody who paid her passage here. She had been injured internally by a kick from a horse; she hadn't a cent on her when she got ashore; I don't think she even asked to see the child. At any rate, not till the last day of her life. Jacobus hired for her a bungalow to die in. He got a couple of Sisters from the hospital to nurse her through these few months. If he didn't marry her *in extremis* as the good Sisters tried to bring about, it's because she wouldn't even hear of it. As the nuns said: 'The

woman died impenitent.' It was reported that she
ordered Jacobus out of the room with her last breath.
This may be the real reason why he didn't go into
mourning himself; he only put the child into black.
While she was little she was to be seen sometimes about
the streets attended by a negro woman, but since she
became of age to put her hair up I don't think she has
set foot outside that garden once. She must be over
eighteen now."

Thus my friend, with some added details; such as,
that he didn't think the girl had spoken to three people
of any position in the island; that an elderly female
relative of the brothers Jacobus had been induced by
extreme poverty to accept the position of gouvernante
to the girl. As to Jacobus's business (which certainly
annoyed his brother) it was a wise choice on his part.
It brought him in contact only with strangers of passage; whereas any other would have given rise to all
sorts of awkwardness with his social equals. The man
was not wanting in a certain tact—only he was naturally
shameless. For why did he want to keep that girl with
him? It was most painful for everybody.

I thought suddenly (and with profound disgust) of
the other Jacobus, and I could not refrain from saying
slily:

"I suppose if he employed her, say, as a scullion in
his household and occasionally pulled her hair or boxed
her ears, the position would have been more regular—
less shocking to the respectable class to which he belongs."

He was not so stupid as to miss my intention, and
shrugged his shoulders impatiently.

"You don't understand. To begin with, she's not
a mulatto. And a scandal is a scandal. People should
be given a chance to forget. I dare say it would have

been better for her if she had been turned into a scullion or something of that kind. Of course he's trying to make money in every sort of petty way, but in such a business there'll never be enough for anybody to come forward."

When my friend left me I had a conception of Jacobus and his daughter existing, a lonely pair of castaways, on a desert island; the girl sheltering in the house as if it were a cavern in a cliff, and Jacobus going out to pick up a living for both on the beach—exactly like two ship-wrecked people who always hope for some rescuer to bring them back at last into touch with the rest of mankind.

But Jacobus's bodily reality did not fit in with this romantic view. When he turned up on board in the usual course, he sipped the cup of coffee placidly, asked me if I was satisfied—and I hardly listened to the harbour gossip he dropped slowly in his low, voice-saving enunciation. I had then troubles of my own. My ship chartered, my thoughts dwelling on the success of a quick round voyage, I had been suddenly confronted by a shortage of bags. A catastrophe! The stock of one especial kind, called pockets, seemed to be totally exhausted. A consignment was shortly expected—it was afloat, on its way, but, meantime, the loading of my ship dead stopped, I had enough to worry about. My consignees, who had received me with such heartiness on my arrival, now, in the character of my charterers, listened to my complaints with polite helplessness. Their manager, the old-maidish, thin man, who so prudishly didn't even like to speak about the impure Jacobus, gave me the correct commercial view of the position.

"My dear Captain"—he was retracting his leathery cheeks into a condescending, shark-like smile—"we were not morally obliged to tell you of a possible shortage before you signed the charter-party. It was for you to guard against the contingency of a delay— strictly speaking. But of course we shouldn't have taken any advantage. This is no one's fault really. We ourselves have been taken unawares," he concluded primly, with an obvious lie.

This lecture I confess had made me thirsty. Suppressed rage generally produces that effect; and as I strolled on aimlessly I bethought myself of the tall earthenware pitcher in the captains' room of the Jacobus "store."

With no more than a nod to the men I found assembled there, I poured down a deep, cool draught on my indignation, then another, and then, becoming dejected, I sat plunged in cheerless reflections. The others read, talked, smoked, bandied over my head some unsubtle chaff. But my abstraction was respected. And it was without a word to any one that I rose and went out, only to be quite unexpectedly accosted in the bustle of the store by Jacobus the outcast.

"Glad to see you, Captain. What? Going away? You haven't been looking so well these last few days, I notice. Run down, eh?"

He was in his shirt-sleeves, and his words were in the usual course of business, but they had a human note. It was commercial amenity, but I had been a stranger to amenity in that connection. I do verily believe (from the direction of his heavy glance towards a certain shelf) that he was going to suggest the purchase of Clarkson's Nerve Tonic, which he kept in stock, when I said impulsively:

"I am rather in trouble with my loading."

Wide awake under his sleepy, broad mask with glued lips, he understood at once, had a movement of the

head so appreciative that I relieved my exasperation
by explaining:

"Surely there must be eleven hundred quarter-bags
to be found in the colony. It's only a matter of looking
for them."

Again that slight movement of the big head, and in
the noise and activity of the store that tranquil murmur:

"To be sure. But then people likely to have a
reserve of quarter-bags wouldn't want to sell. They'd
need that size themselves."

"That's exactly what my consignees are telling me.
Impossible to buy. Bosh! They don't want to. It
suits them to have the ship hung up. But if I were to
discover the lot they would have to—— Look here,
Jacobus! *You* are the man to have such a thing up
your sleeve."

He protested with a ponderous swing of his big head.
I stood before him helplessly, being looked at by those
heavy eyes with a veiled expression as of a man after
some soul-shaking crisis. Then, suddenly:

"It's impossible to talk quietly here," he whispered.
"I am very busy. But if you could go and wait for
me in my house. It's less than ten minutes' walk.
Oh, yes, you don't know the way."

He called for his coat and offered to take me there
himself. He would have to return to the store at once
for an hour or so to finish his business, and then he
would be at liberty to talk over with me that matter of
quarter-bags. This programme was breathed out at
me through slightly parted, still lips; his heavy, motionless glance rested upon me, placid as ever, the glance of
a tired man—but I felt that it was searching, too. I
could not imagine what he was looking for in me and
kept silent, wondering.

"I am asking you to wait for me in my house

till I am at liberty to talk this matter over. You will?"

"Why, of course!" I cried.

"But I cannot promise——"

"I dare say not," I said. "I don't expect a promise."

"I mean I can't even promise to try the move I've in my mind. One must see first . . . h'm!"

"All right. I'll take the chance. I'll wait for you as long as you like. What else have I to do in this infernal hole of a port!"

Before I had uttered my last words we had set off at a swinging pace. We turned a couple of corners and entered a street completely empty of traffic, of semi-rural aspect, paved with cobblestones nestling in grass tufts. The house came to the line of the roadway; a single story on an elevated basement of rough-stones, so that our heads were below the level of the windows as we went along. All the jalousies were tightly shut, like eyes, and the house seemed fast asleep in the afternoon sunshine. The entrance was at the side, in an alley even more grass-grown than the street: a small door, simply on the latch.

With a word of apology as to showing me the way, Jacobus preceded me up a dark passage and led me across the naked parquet floor of what I supposed to be the dining room. It was lighted by three glass doors which stood wide open on to a verandah or rather loggia running its brick arches along the garden side of the house. It was really a magnificent garden: smooth green lawns and a gorgeous maze of flower-beds in the foreground, displayed around a basin of dark water framed in a marble rim, and in the distance the massed foliage of varied trees concealing the roofs of other houses. The town might have been miles away. It was a brilliantly coloured solitude, drowsing in a warm,

voluptuous silence. Where the long, still shadows fell
across the beds, and in shady nooks, the massed colours
of the flowers had an extraordinary magnificence of
effect. I stood entranced. Jacobus grasped me delicately above the elbow, impelling me to a half-turn to
the left.

I had not noticed the girl before. She occupied a
low, deep, wickerwork arm-chair, and I saw her in
exact profile like a figure in a tapestry, and as motionless.
Jacobus released my arm.

"This is Alice," he announced tranquilly; and his
subdued manner of speaking made it sound so much
like a confidential communication that I fancied myself nodding understandingly and whispering: "I see,
I see." . . . Of course, I did nothing of the kind.
Neither of us did anything; we stood side by side looking
down at the girl. For quite a time she did not stir,
staring straight before her as if watching the vision of
some pageant passing through the garden in the deep,
rich glow of light and the splendour of flowers.

Then, coming to the end of her reverie, she looked
round and up. If I had not at first noticed her, I
am certain that she too had been unaware of my
presence till she actually perceived me by her father's
side. The quickened upward movement of the heavy
eyelids, the widening of the languid glance, passing into
a fixed stare, put that beyond doubt.

Under her amazement there was a hint of fear, and
then came a flash as of anger. Jacobus, after uttering
my name fairly loud, said: "Make yourself at home,
Captain—I won't be gone long," and went away rapidly.
Before I had time to make a bow I was left alone with
the girl—who, I remembered suddenly, had not been
seen by any man or woman of that town since she had
found it necessary to put up her hair. It looked as

though it had not been touched again since that distant time of first putting up; it was a mass of black, lustrous locks, twisted anyhow high on her head, with long, untidy wisps hanging down on each side of the clear sallow face; a mass so thick and strong and abundant that, nothing but to look at, it gave you a sensation of heavy pressure on the top of your head and an impression of magnificently cynical untidiness. She leaned forward, hugging herself with crossed legs; a dingy, amber-coloured, flounced wrapper of some thin stuff revealed the young supple body drawn together tensely in the deep low seat as if crouching for a spring. I detected a slight, quivering start or two, which looked uncommonly like bounding away. They were followed by the most absolute immobility.

The absurd impulse to run out after Jacobus (for I had been startled, too) once repressed, I took a chair, placed it not very far from her, sat down deliberately, and began to talk about the garden, caring not what I said, but using a gentle caressing intonation as one talks to soothe a startled wild animal. I could not even be certain that she understood me. She never raised her face nor attempted to look my way. I kept on talking only to prevent her from taking flight. She had another of those quivering, repressed starts which made me catch my breath with apprehension.

Ultimately I formed a notion that what prevented her perhaps from going off in one great, nervous leap, was the scantiness of her attire. The wicker arm-chair was the most substantial thing about her person. What she had on under that dingy, loose, amber wrapper must have been of the most flimsy and airy character. One could not help being aware of it. It was obvious. I felt it actually embarrassing at first; but that sort of embarrassment is got over easily by a mind not enslaved by narrow prejudices. I did not avert my gaze from Alice. I went on talking with ingratiating softness, the recollection that, most likely, she had never before been spoken to by a strange man adding to my assurance. I don't know why an emotional tenseness should have crept into the situation. But it did. And just as I was becoming aware of it a slight scream cut short my flow of urbane speech.

The scream did not proceed from the girl. It was emitted behind me, and caused me to turn my head sharply. I understood at once that the apparition in the doorway was the elderly relation of Jacobus, the companion, the gouvernante. While she remained thunderstruck, I got up and made her a low bow.

The ladies of Jacobus's household evidently spent their days in light attire. This stumpy old woman with a face like a large wrinkled lemon, beady eyes, and a shock of iron-grey hair, was dressed in a garment of some ash-coloured, silky, light stuff. It fell from her thick neck down to her toes with the simplicity of an unadorned nightgown. It made her appear truly cylindrical. She exclaimed: "How did you get here?"

Before I could say a word she vanished and presently I heard a confusion of shrill protestations in a distant part of the house. Obviously no one could tell her how I got there. In a moment, with great outcries from two negro women following her, she waddled back to the doorway, infuriated.

"What do you want here?"

I turned to the girl. She was sitting straight up now, her hands posed on the arms of the chair. I appealed to her.

"Surely, Miss Alice, you will not let them drive me out into the street?"

Her magnificent black eyes, narrowed, long in shape,

swept over me with an indefinable expression, then in a harsh, contemptuous voice she let fall in French a sort of explanation:

"*C'est papa.*"

I made another low bow to the old woman.

She turned her back on me in order to drive away her black henchwomen, then surveying my person in a peculiar manner with one small eye nearly closed and her face all drawn up on that side as if with a twinge of toothache, she stepped out on the verandah, sat down in a rocking-chair some distance away, and took up her knitting from a little table. Before she started at it she plunged one of the needles into the mop of her grey hair and stirred it vigorously.

Her elementary nightgown-sort of frock clung to her ancient, stumpy, and floating form. She wore white cotton stockings and flat brown velvet slippers. Her feet and ankles were obtrusively visible on the foot-rest. She began to rock herself slightly, while she knitted. I had resumed my seat and kept quiet, for I mistrusted that old woman. What if she ordered me to depart? She seemed capable of any outrage. She had snorted once or twice; she was knitting violently. Suddenly she piped at the young girl in French a question which I translate colloquially:

"What's your father up to, now?"

The young creature shrugged her shoulders so comprehensively that her whole body swayed within the loose wrapper; and in that unexpectedly harsh voice which yet had a seductive quality to the senses, like certain kinds of natural rough wines one drinks with pleasure.

"It's some captain. Leave me alone—will you!"

The chair rocked quicker, the old, thin voice was like a whistle.

"You and your father make a pair. He would stick at nothing—that's well known. But I didn't expect this."

I thought it high time to air some of my own French. I remarked modestly, but firmly, that this was business. I had some matters to talk over with Mr. Jacobus.

At once she piped out a derisive "Poor innocent!" Then, with a change of tone: "The shop's for business. Why don't you go to the shop to talk with him?"

The furious speed of her fingers and knitting-needles made one dizzy; and with squeaky indignation:

"Sitting here staring at that girl—is that what you call business?"

"No," I said suavely. "I call this pleasure—an unexpected pleasure. And unless Miss Alice objects—— "

I half turned to her. She flung at me an angry and contemptuous "Don't care!" and leaning her elbow on her knees took her chin in her hand—a Jacobus chin undoubtedly. And those heavy eyelids, this black irritated stare reminded me of Jacobus, too—the wealthy merchant, the respected one. The design of her eyebrows also was the same, rigid and ill-omened. Yes! I traced in her a resemblance to both of them. It came to me as a sort of surprising remote inference that both these Jacobuses were rather handsome men after all. I said:

"Oh! Then I shall stare at you till you smile."

She favoured me again with an even more viciously scornful "Don't care!"

The old woman broke in blunt and shrill:

"Hear his impudence! And you too! Don't care! Go at least and put some more clothes on. Sitting there like this before this sailor riff-raff."

The sun was about to leave the Pearl of the Ocean for other seas, for other lands. The walled garden full of shadows blazed with colour as if the flowers were giving up the light absorbed during the day. The amazing old woman became very explicit. She suggested to the girl a corset and a petticoat with a cynical unreserve which humiliated me. Was I of no more account than a wooden dummy? The girl snapped out: "Shan't!"

It was not the naughty retort of a vulgar child; it had a note of desperation. Clearly my intrusion had somehow upset the balance of their established relations. The old woman knitted with furious accuracy, her eyes fastened down on her work.

"Oh, you are the true child of your father! And *that* talks of entering a convent! Letting herself be stared at by a fellow."

"Leave off."

"Shameless thing!"

"Old sorceress," the girl uttered distinctly, preserving her meditative pose, chin in hand, and a far-away stare over the garden.

It was like the quarrel of the kettle and the pot. The old woman flew out of the chair, banged down her work, and with a great play of thick limb perfectly visible in that weird, clinging garment of hers, strode at the girl—who never stirred. I was experiencing a sort of trepidation when, as if awed by that unconscious attitude, the aged relative of Jacobus turned short upon me.

She was, I perceived, armed with a knitting-needle; and as she raised her hand her intention seemed to be to throw it at me like a dart. But she only used it to scratch her head with, examining me the while at close range, one eye nearly shut and her face distorted by a whimsical, one-sided grimace.

"My dear man," she asked abruptly, "do you expect any good to come of this?"

"I do hope so indeed, Miss Jacobus." I tried to speak in the easy tone of an afternoon caller. "You see, I am here after some bags."

"Bags! Look at that now! Didn't I hear you holding forth to that graceless wretch?"

"You would like to see me in my grave," uttered the motionless girl hoarsely.

"Grave! What about me? Buried alive before I am dead for the sake of a thing blessed with such a pretty father!" she cried; and turning to me: "You're one of those men he does business with. Well—why don't you leave us in peace, my good fellow?"

It was said in a tone—this "leave us in peace." There was a sort of ruffianly familiarity, a superiority, a scorn in it. I was to hear it more than once, for you would show an imperfect knowledge of human nature if you thought that this was my last visit to that house— where no respectable person had put foot for ever so many years. No, you would be very much mistaken if you imagined that this reception had scared me away. First of all I was not going to run before a grotesque and ruffianly old woman.

And then you mustn't forget these necessary bags. That first evening Jacobus made me stay to dinner; after, however, telling me loyally that he didn't know whether he could do anything at all for me. He had been thinking it over. It was too difficult, he feared. . . . But he did not give it up in so many words.

We were only three at table; the girl by means of repeated "Won't!" "Shan't!" and "Don't care!" having conveyed and affirmed her intention not to come to the table, not to have any dinner, not to move from the verandah. The old relative hopped about in her flat slippers and piped indignantly, Jacobus towered over her and murmured placidly in his throat; I joined jocularly from a distance, throwing in a few words, for which under the cover of the night I received secretly a most vicious poke in the ribs from the old woman's elbow or perhaps her fist. I restrained a cry. And all the time the girl didn't even condescend to raise her head to look at any of us. All this may sound childish—and yet that stony, petulant sullenness had an obscurely tragic flavour.

And so we sat down to the food around the light of a good many candles while she remained crouching out there, staring in the dark as if feeding her bad temper on the heavily scented air of the admirable garden.

Before leaving I said to Jacobus that I would come next day to hear if the bag affair had made any progress. He shook his head slightly at that.

"I'll haunt your house daily till you pull it off. You'll be always finding me here."

His faint, melancholy smile did not part his thick lips.

"That will be all right, Captain."

Then seeing me to the door, very tranquil, he murmured earnestly the recommendation: "Make yourself at home," and also the hospitable hint about there being always "a plate of soup." It was only on my way to the quay, down the ill-lighted streets, that I remembered I had been engaged to dine that very evening with the S—— family. Though vexed with my forgetfulness (it would be rather awkward to explain) I couldn't help thinking that it had procured me a more amusing evening. And besides—business. The sacred business——.

In a barefooted negro who overtook me at a run and bolted down the landing-steps I recognised Jacobus's boatman, who must have been feeding in the kitchen. His usual "Good-night, sah!" as I went up my ship's

ladder had a more cordial sound than on previous
occasions.

V

I KEPT my word to Jacobus. I haunted his home.
He was perpetually finding me there of an afternoon
when he popped in for a moment from the "store."
The sound of my voice talking to his Alice greeted him
on his doorstep; and when he returned for good in the
evening, ten to one he would hear it still going on in
the verandah. I just nodded to him; he would sit down
heavily and gently, and watch with a sort of approving
anxiety my efforts to make his daughter smile.

I called her often "Alice," right before him; sometimes I would address her as Miss "Don't Care," and
I exhausted myself in nonsensical chatter without
succeeding once in taking her out of her peevish and
tragic self. There were moments when I felt I must
break out and start swearing at her till all was blue.
And I fancied that had I done so Jacobus would not
have moved a muscle. A sort of shady, intimate understanding seemed to have been established between us.

I must say the girl treated her father exactly in the
same way she treated me.

And how could it have been otherwise? She treated
me as she treated her father. She had never seen a
visitor. She did not know how men behaved. I belonged to the low lot with whom her father did business
at the port. I was of no account. So was her father.
The only decent people in the world were the people of
the island, who would have nothing to do with him because of something wicked he had done. This was
apparently the explanation Miss Jacobus had given her
of the household's isolated position. For she had to be

told something! And I feel convinced that this version had been assented to by Jacobus. I must say the old woman was putting it forward with considerable gusto. It was on her lips the universal explanation, the universal allusion, the universal taunt.

One day Jacobus came in early and, beckoning me into the dining-room, wiped his brow with a weary gesture and told me that he had managed to unearth a supply of quarter-bags.

"It's fourteen hundred your ship wanted, did you say, Captain?"

"Yes, yes!" I replied eagerly; but he remained calm. He looked more tired than I had ever seen him before.

"Well, Captain, you may go and tell your people that they can get that lot from my brother."

As I remained open-mouthed at this, he added his usual placid formula of assurance:

"You'll find it correct, Captain."

"You spoke to your brother about it?" I was distinctly awed. "And for me? Because he must have known that my ship's the only one hung up for bags. How on earth——"

He wiped his brow again. I noticed that he was dressed with unusual care, in clothes in which I had never seen him before. He avoided my eye.

"You've heard people talk, of course. . . . That's true enough. He . . . I . . . We certainly . . . for several years . . ." His voice declined to a mere sleepy murmur. "You see I had something to tell him of, something which——"

His murmur stopped. He was not going to tell me what this something was. And I didn't care. Anxious to carry the news to my charterers, I ran back on the verandah to get my hat.

At the bustle I made the girl turned her eyes slowly

in my direction, and even the old woman was checked in her knitting. I stopped a moment to exclaim excitedly:

"Your father's a brick, Miss Don't Care. That's what he is."

She beheld my elation in scornful surprise. Jacobus with unwonted familiarity seized my arm as I flew through the dining-room, and breathed heavily at me a proposal about "A plate of soup" that evening. I answered distractedly: "Eh? What? Oh, thanks! Certainly. With pleasure," and tore myself away. Dine with him? Of course. The merest gratitude——

But some three hours afterwards, in the dusky, silent street, paved with cobble-stones, I became aware that it was not mere gratitude which was guiding my steps towards the house with the old garden, where for years no guest other than myself had ever dined. Mere gratitude does not gnaw at one's interior economy in that particular way. Hunger might; but I was not feeling particularly hungry for Jacobus's food.

On that occasion, too, the girl refused to come to the table.

My exasperation grew. The old woman cast malicious glances at me. I said suddenly to Jacobus: "Here! Put some chicken and salad on that plate." He obeyed without raising his eyes. I carried it with a knife and fork and a serviette out on the verandah. The garden was one mass of gloom, like a cemetery of flowers buried in the darkness, and she, in the chair, seemed to muse mournfully over the extinction of light and colour. Only whiffs of heavy scent passed like wandering, fragrant souls of that departed multitude of blossoms. I talked volubly, jocularly, persuasively, tenderly; I talked in a subdued tone. To a listener it would have sounded like the murmur of a pleading lover. Whenever I paused expectantly there was only a deep silence. It was like offering food to a seated statue.

"I haven't been able to swallow a single morsel thinking of you out here starving yourself in the dark. It's positively cruel to be so obstinate. Think of my sufferings."

"Don't care."

I felt as if I could have done her some violence— shaken her, beaten her maybe. I said:

"Your absurd behaviour will prevent me coming here any more."

"What's that to me?"

"You like it."

"It's false," she snarled.

My hand fell on her shoulder; and if she had flinched I verily believe I would have shaken her. But there was no movement and this immobility disarmed my anger.

"You do. Or you wouldn't be found on the verandah every day. Why are you here, then? There are plenty of rooms in the house. You have your own room to stay in—if you did not want to see me. But you do. You know you do."

I felt a slight shudder under my hand and released my grip as if frightened by that sign of animation in her body. The scented air of the garden came to us in a warm wave like a voluptuous and perfumed sigh.

"Go back to them," she whispered, almost pitifully.

As I re-entered the dining-room I saw Jacobus cast down his eyes. I banged the plate on the table. At this demonstration of ill-humour he murmured something in an apologetic tone, and I turned on him viciously as if he were accountable to me for these "abominable eccentricities," I believe I called them.

"But I dare say Miss Jacobus here is responsible for most of this offensive manner," I added loftily.

She piped out at once in her brazen, ruffianly manner:

"Eh? Why don't you leave us in peace, my good fellow?"

I was astonished that she should dare before Jacobus. Yet what could he have done to repress her? He needed her too much. He raised a heavy, drowsy glance for an instant, then looked down again. She insisted with shrill finality:

"Haven't you done your business, you two? Well, then——"

She had the true Jacobus impudence, that old woman. Her mop of iron-grey hair was parted on the side like a man's, raffishly, and she made as if to plunge her fork into it, as she used to do with the knitting-needle, but refrained. Her little black eyes sparkled venomously. I turned to my host at the head of the table—menacingly as it were.

"Well, and what do you say to that, Jacobus? Am I to take it that we have done with each other?"

I had to wait a little. The answer when it came was rather unexpected, and in quite another spirit than the question.

"I certainly think we might do some business yet with those potatoes of mine, Captain. You will find that——"

I cut him short.

"I've told you before that I don't trade."

His broad chest heaved without a sound in a noiseless sigh.

"Think it over, Captain," he murmured, tenacious and tranquil; and I burst into a jarring laugh, re-

membering how he had stuck to the circus-rider woman
—the depth of passion under that placid surface, which
even cuts with a riding-whip (so the legend had it)
could never ruffle into the semblance of a storm; something like the passion of a fish would be if one could
imagine such a thing as a passionate fish.

That evening I experienced more distinctly than ever
the sense of moral discomfort which always attended
me in that house lying under the ban of all "decent"
people. I refused to stay on and smoke after dinner;
and when I put my hand into the thickly cushioned
palm of Jacobus, I said to myself that it would be for
the last time under his roof. I pressed his bulky paw
heartily nevertheless. Hadn't he got me out of a
serious difficulty? To the few words of acknowledge-
ment I was bound, and indeed quite willing, to utter, he
answered by stretching his closed lips in his melancholy,
glued-together smile.

"That will be all right, I hope, Captain," he breathed
out weightily.

"What do you mean?" I asked, alarmed. "That
your brother might yet——"

"Oh, no," he reassured me. "He . . . he's a
man of his word, Captain."

My self-communion as I walked away from his door,
trying to believe that this was for the last time, was not
satisfactory. I was aware myself that I was not
sincere in my reflections as to Jacobus's motives, and,
of course, the very next day I went back again.

How weak, irrational, and absurd we are! How
easily carried away whenever our awakened imagination brings us the irritating hint of a desire! I cared
for the girl in a particular way, seduced by the moody
expression of her face, by her obstinate silences, her
rare, scornful words; by the perpetual pout of her closed

lips, the black depths of her fixed gaze turned slowly upon me as if in contemptuous provocation, only to be averted next moment with an exasperating indifference.

Of course the news of my assiduity had spread all over the little town. I noticed a change in the manner of my acquaintances and even something different in the nods of the other captains, when meeting them at the landing-steps or in the offices where business called me. The old-maidish head clerk treated me with distant punctiliousness and, as it were, gathered his skirts round him for fear of contamination. It seemed to me that the very niggers on the quays turned to look after me as I passed; and as to Jacobus's boatman his "Good-night sah!" when he put me on board was no longer merely cordial—it had a familiar, confidential sound as though we had been partners in some villainy.

My friend S—— the elder passed me on the other side of the street with a wave of the hand and an ironic smile. The younger brother, the one they had married to an elderly shrew, he, on the strength of an older friendship and as if paying a debt of gratitude, took the liberty to utter a word of warning.

"You're doing yourself no good by your choice of friends, my dear chap," he said with infantile gravity.

As I knew that the meeting of the brothers Jacobus was the subject of excited comment in the whole of the sugary Pearl of the Ocean I wanted to know why I was blamed.

"I have been the occasion of a move which may end in a reconciliation surely desirable from the point of view of the proprieties—don't you know?"

"Of course, if that girl were disposed of it would certainly facilitate——" he mused sagely, then, inconsequential creature, gave me a light tap on the lower part of my waistcoat. "You old sinner," he cried jovially, "much you care for proprieties. But you had better look out for yourself, you know, with a personage like Jacobus who has no sort of reputation to lose."

He had recovered his gravity of a respectable citizen by that time and added regretfully:

"All the women of our family are perfectly scandalized."

But by that time I had given up visiting the S—— family and the D—— family. The elder ladies pulled such faces when I showed myself, and the multitude of related young ladies received me with such a variety of looks: wondering, awed, mocking (except Miss Mary, who spoke to me and looked at me with hushed, pained compassion as though I had been ill), that I had no difficulty in giving them all up. I would have given up the society of the whole town, for the sake of sitting near that girl, snarling and superb and barely clad in that flimsy, dingy, amber wrapper, open low at the throat. She looked, with the wild wisps of hair hanging down her tense face, as though she had just jumped out of bed in the panic of a fire.

She sat leaning on her elbow, looking at nothing. Why did she stay listening to my absurd chatter? And not only that; but why did she powder her face in preparation for my arrival? It seemed to be her idea of making a toilette, and in her untidy negligence a sign of great effort towards personal adornment.

But I might have been mistaken. The powdering might have been her daily practice and her presence in the verandah a sign of an indifference so complete as to take no account of my existence. Well, it was all one to me.

I loved to watch her slow changes of pose, to look at

her long immobilities composed in the graceful lines of
her body, to observe the mysterious narrow stare of her
splendid black eyes, somewhat long in shape, half
closed, contemplating the void. She was like a spell-
bound creature with the forehead of a goddess crowned
by the dishevelled magnificent hair of a gipsy tramp.
Even her indifference was seductive. I felt myself
growing attached to her by the bond of an irrealizable
desire, for I kept my head—quite. And I put up with
the moral discomfort of Jacobus's sleepy watchfulness,
tranquil, and yet so expressive; as if there had been a
tacit pact between us two. I put up with the insolence of the old woman's: "Aren't you ever going
to leave us in peace, my good fellow?" with her taunts;
with her brazen and sinister scolding. She was of the
true Jacobus stock, and no mistake.

Directly I got away from the girl I called myself
many hard names. What folly was this? I would
ask myself. It was like being the slave of some
depraved habit. And I returned to her with my
head clear, my heart certainly free, not even moved
by pity for that castaway (she was as much of a
castaway as any one ever wrecked on a desert island),
but as if beguiled by some extraordinary promise.
Nothing more unworthy could be imagined. The
recollection of that tremulous whisper when I gripped
her shoulder with one hand and held a plate of chicken
with the other was enough to make me break all my
good resolutions.

Her insulting taciturnity was enough sometimes to
make one gnash one's teeth with rage. When she
opened her mouth it was only to be abominably rude
in harsh tones to the associate of her reprobate father;
and the full approval of her aged relative was conveyed
to her by offensive chuckles. If not that, then her

remarks, always uttered in the tone of scathing contempt, were of the most appalling inanity.

How could it have been otherwise? That plump, ruffianly Jacobus old maid in the tight grey frock had never taught her any manners. Manners I suppose are not necessary for born castaways. No educational establishment could ever be induced to accept her as a pupil—on account of the proprieties, I imagine. And Jacobus had not been able to send her away anywhere. How could he have done it? Whom with? Where to? He himself was not enough of an adventurer to think of settling down anywhere else. His passion had tossed him at the tail of a circus up and down strange coasts, but, the storm over, he had drifted back shamelessly where, social outcast as he was, he remained still a Jacobus—one of the oldest families on the island, older than the French even. There must have been a Jacobus in at the death of the last Dodo. . . . The girl had learned nothing, she had never listened to a general conversation, she knew nothing, she had heard of nothing. She could read certainly; but all the reading matter that ever came in her way were the newspapers provided for the captains' room of the "store." Jacobus had the habit of taking these sheets home now and then in a very stained and ragged condition.

As her mind could not grasp the meaning of any matters treated there except police-court reports and accounts of crimes, she had formed for herself a notion of the civilised world as a scene of murders, abductions, burglaries, stabbing affrays, and every sort of desperate violence. England and France, Paris and London (the only two towns of which she seemed to have heard), appeared to her sinks of abomination, reeking with blood, in contrast to her little island where petty larceny was about the standard of current misdeeds, with, now and then, some more pronounced crime— and that only amongst the imported coolie labourers on sugar estates or the negroes of the town. But in Europe these things were being done daily by a wicked population of white men amongst whom, as that ruffianly, aristocratic old Miss Jacobus pointed out, the wandering sailors, the associates of her precious papa, were the lowest of the low.

It was impossible to give her a sense of proportion. I suppose she figured England to herself as about the size of the Pearl of the Ocean; in which case it would certainly have been reeking with gore and a mere wreck of burgled houses from end to end. One could not make her understand that these horrors on which she fed her imagination were lost in the mass of orderly life like a few drops of blood in the ocean. She directed upon me for a moment the uncomprehending glance of her narrowed eyes and then would turn her scornful powdered face away without a word. She would not even take the trouble to shrug her shoulders.

At that time the batches of papers brought by the last mail reported a series of crimes in the East End of London, there was a sensational case of abduction in France and a fine display of armed robbery in Australia. One afternoon crossing the dining-room I heard Miss Jacobus piping in the verandah with venomous animosity: "I don't know what your precious papa is plotting with that fellow. But he's just the sort of man who's capable of carrying you off far away somewhere and then cutting your throat some day for your money."

There was a good half of the length of the verandah between their chairs. I came out and sat down fiercely midway between them.

"Yes, that's what we do with girls in Europe," I began in a grimly matter-of-fact tone. I think Miss Jacobus was disconcerted by my sudden appearance. I turned upon her with cold ferocity:

"As to objectionable old women, they are first strangled quietly, then cut up into small pieces and thrown away, a bit here and a bit there. They vanish——"

I cannot go so far as to say I had terrified her. But she was troubled by my truculence, the more so because I had been always addressing her with a politeness she did not deserve. Her plump, knitting hands fell slowly on her knees. She said not a word while I fixed her with severe determination. Then as I turned away from her at last, she laid down her work gently and, with noiseless movements, retreated from the verandah. In fact, she vanished.

But I was not thinking of her. I was looking at the girl. It was what I was coming for daily; troubled, ashamed, eager; finding in my nearness to her a unique sensation which I indulged with dread, self-contempt, and deep pleasure, as if it were a secret vice bound to end in my undoing, like the habit of some drug or other which ruins and degrades its slave.

I looked her over, from the top of her dishevelled head, down the lovely line of the shoulder, following the curve of the hip, the draped form of the long limb, right down to her fine ankle below a torn, soiled flounce; and as far as the point of the shabby, high-heeled, blue slipper, dangling from her well-shaped foot, which she moved slightly, with quick, nervous jerks, as if impatient of my presence. And in the scent of the massed flowers I seemed to breathe her special and inexplicable charm, the heady perfume of the everlastingly irritated captive of the garden.

I looked at her rounded chin, the Jacobus chin; at the full, red lips pouting in the powdered, sallow face; at the firm modelling of the cheek, the grains of white in the hairs of the straight sombre eyebrows; at the long eyes, a narrowed gleam of liquid white and intense motionless black, with their gaze so empty of thought, and so absorbed in their fixity that she seemed to be staring at her own lonely image, in some far-off mirror hidden from my sight amongst the trees.

And suddenly, without looking at me, with the appearance of a person speaking to herself, she asked, in that voice slightly harsh yet mellow and always irritated:

"Why do you keep on coming here?"

"Why do I keep on coming here?" I repeated, taken by surprise. I could not have told her. I could not even tell myself with sincerity why I was coming there. "What's the good of you asking a question like that?"

"Nothing is any good," she observed scornfully to the empty air, her chin propped on her hand, that hand never extended to any man, that no one had ever grasped—for I had only grasped her shoulder once—that generous, fine, somewhat masculine hand. I knew well the peculiarly efficient shape—broad at the base, tapering at the fingers—of that hand, for which there was nothing in the world to lay hold of. I pretended to be playful.

"No! But do you really care to know?"

She shrugged indolently her magnificent shoulders, from which the dingy thin wrapper was slipping a little.

"Oh—never mind—never mind!"

There was something smouldering under those airs of lassitude. She exasperated me by the provocation of her nonchalance, by something elusive and defiant in her very form which I wanted to seize. I said roughly:

"Why? Don't you think I should tell you the truth?"

Her eyes glided my way for a sidelong look, and she murmured, moving only her full, pouting lips:

"I think you would not dare."

"Do you imagine I am afraid of you? What on earth. . . . Well, it's possible, after all, that I don't know exactly why I am coming here. Let us say, with Miss Jacobus, that it is for no good. You seem to believe the outrageous things she says, if you do have a row with her now and then."

She snapped out viciously:

"Who else am I to believe?"

"I don't know," I had to own, seeing her suddenly very helpless and condemned to moral solitude by the verdict of a respectable community. "You might believe me, if you chose."

She made a slight movement and asked me at once, with an effort as if making an experiment:

"What is the business between you and papa?"

"Don't you know the nature of your father's business? Come! He sells provisions to ships."

She became rigid again in her crouching pose.

"Not that. What brings you here—to this house?"

"And suppose it's you? You would not call that business? Would you? And now let us drop the subject. It's no use. My ship will be ready for sea the day after to-morrow."

She murmured a distinctly scared "So soon," and getting up quickly, went to the little table and poured herself a glass of water. She walked with rapid steps and with an indolent swaying of her whole young figure above the hips; when she passed near me I felt with tenfold force the charm of the peculiar, promising sensation I had formed the habit to seek near her. I thought with sudden dismay that this was the end of it; that after one more day I would be no longer able to come into this verandah, sit on this chair, and taste perversely the flavour of contempt in her indolent poses, drink in the provocation of her scornful looks, and listen to the curt, insolent remarks uttered in that harsh and seductive voice. As if my innermost nature had been altered by the action of some moral poison, I felt an abject dread of going to sea.

I had to exercise a sudden self-control, as one puts on a brake, to prevent myself jumping up to stride about, shout, gesticulate, make her a scene. What for? What about? I had no idea. It was just the relief of violence that I wanted; and I lolled back in my chair, trying to keep my lips formed in a smile; that half-indulgent, half-mocking smile which was my shield against the shafts of her contempt and the insulting sallies flung at me by the old woman.

She drank the water at a draught, with the avidity of raging thirst, and let herself fall on the nearest chair, as if utterly overcome. Her attitude, like certain tones of her voice, had in it something masculine: the knees apart in the ample wrapper, the clasped hands hanging between them, her body leaning forward, with drooping head. I stared at the heavy black coil of twisted hair. It was enormous, crowning the bowed head with a crushing and disdained glory. The escaped wisps hung straight down. And suddenly I perceived that the girl was trembling from head to foot, as though that glass of iced water had chilled her to the bone.

"What's the matter now?" I said, startled, but in no very sympathetic mood.

She shook her bowed, overweighted head and cried in a stifled voice but with a rising inflection:

"Go away! Go away! Go away!"

I got up then and approached her, with a strange sort of anxiety. I looked down at her round, strong neck, then stooped low enough to peep at her face. And I began to tremble a little myself.

"What on earth are you gone wild about, Miss Don't Care?"

She flung herself backwards violently, her head going over the back of the chair. And now it was her smooth, full, palpitating throat that lay exposed to my bewildered stare. Her eyes were nearly closed, with only a horrible white gleam under the lids as if she were dead.

"What has come to you?" I asked in awe. "What are you terrifying yourself with?"

She pulled herself together, her eyes open frightfully wide now. The tropical afternoon was lengthening the shadows on the hot, weary earth, the abode of obscure desires, of extravagant hopes, of unimaginable terrors.

"Never mind! Don't care!" Then, after a gasp, she spoke with such frightful rapidity that I could hardly make out the amazing words: "For if you were to shut me up in an empty place as smooth all round as the palm of my hand, I could always strangle myself with my hair."

For a moment, doubting my ears, I let this inconceivable declaration sink into me. It is ever impossible to guess at the wild thoughts that pass through the heads of our fellow-creatures. What monstrous imaginings of violence could have dwelt under the low forehead of that girl who had been taught to regard her father as "capable of anything" more in the light of a misfortune than that of a disgrace; as, evidently, something to be resented and feared rather than to be ashamed of? She seemed, indeed, as unaware of shame as of anything else in the world; but in her ignorance, her resentment and fear took a childish and violent shape.

Of course she spoke without knowing the value of words. What could she know of death—she who knew nothing of life? It was merely as the proof of her being beside herself with some odious apprehension, that this extraordinary speech had moved me, not to pity, but to a fascinated, horrified wonder. I had no idea what notion she had of her danger. Some sort of abduction. It was quite possible with the talk of that atrocious old woman. Perhaps she thought she could be carried off, bound hand and foot and even gagged. At that surmise I felt as if the door of a furnace had been opened in front of me.

"Upon my honour!" I cried. "You will end by going crazy if you listen to that abominable old aunt of yours——"

I studied her haggard expression, her trembling lips. Her cheeks even seemed sunk a little. But how I, the associate of her disreputable father, the "lowest of the low" from the criminal Europe, could manage to reassure her I had no conception. She was exasperating.

"Heavens and earth! What do you think I can do?"

"I don't know."

Her chin certainly trembled. And she was looking at me with extreme attention. I made a step nearer to her chair.

"I shall do nothing. I promise you that. Will that do? Do you understand? I shall do nothing whatever, of any kind; and the day after to-morrow I shall be gone."

What else could I have said? She seemed to drink
in my words with the thirsty avidity with which she
had emptied the glass of water. She whispered tremulously, in that touching tone I had heard once before on
her lips, and which thrilled me again with the same
emotion:

"I would believe you. But what about papa——"

"He be hanged!" My emotion betrayed itself by
the brutality of my tone. "I've had enough of your
papa. Are you so stupid as to imagine that I am
frightened of him? He can't make me do anything."

All that sounded feeble to me in the face of her
ignorance. But I must conclude that the "accent of
sincerity" has, as some people say, a really irresistible
power. The effect was far beyond my hopes—and
even beyond my conception. To watch the change in
the girl was like watching a miracle—the gradual but
swift relaxation of her tense glance, of her stiffened
muscles, of every fibre of her body. That black, fixed
stare into which I had read a tragic meaning more
than once, in which I had found a sombre seduction,
was perfectly empty now, void of all consciousness
whatever, and not even aware any longer of my presence; it had become a little sleepy, in the Jacobus
fashion.

But, man being a perverse animal, instead of rejoicing
at my complete success, I beheld it with astounded and
indignant eyes. There was something cynical in that
unconcealed alteration, the true Jacobus shamelessness.
I felt as though I had been cheated in some rather
complicated deal into which I had entered against my
better judgment. Yes, cheated without any regard for,
at least, the forms of decency.

With an easy, indolent, and in its indolence supple,
feline movement, she rose from the chair, so provok-

ingly ignoring me now, that for very rage I held my
ground within less than a foot of her. Leisurely and
tranquil, behaving right before me with the ease of a
person alone in a room, she extended her beautiful
arms, with her hands clenched, her body swaying, her
head thrown back a little, revelling contemptuously in
a sense of relief, easing her limbs in freedom after all
these days of crouching, motionless poses when she had
been so furious and so afraid.

All this with supreme indifference, incredible, offensive, exasperating, like ingratitude doubled with
treachery.

I ought to have been flattered, perhaps, but, on the
contrary, my anger grew; her movement to pass by me
as if I were a wooden post or a piece of furniture, that
unconcerned movement brought it to a head.

I won't say I did not know what I was doing, but,
certainly, cool reflection had nothing to do with the
circumstance that next moment both my arms were
round her waist. It was an impulsive action, as one
snatches at something falling or escaping; and it had no
hypocritical gentleness about it either. She had no
time to make a sound, and the first kiss I planted on her
closed lips was vicious enough to have been a bite.

She did not resist, and of course I did not stop at
one. She let me go on, not as if she were inanimate
—I felt her there, close against me, young, full of
vigour, of life, a strong desirable creature, but as if
she did not care in the least, in the absolute assurance
of her safety, what I did or left undone. Our faces
brought close together in this storm of haphazard
caresses, her big, black, wide-open eyes looked into
mine without the girl appearing either angry or pleased
or moved in any way. In that steady gaze which
seemed impersonally to watch my madness I could

detect a slight surprise, perhaps—nothing more. I showered kisses upon her face and there did not seem to be any reason why this should not go on for ever.

That thought flashed through my head, and I was on the point of desisting, when, all at once, she began to struggle with a sudden violence which all but freed her instantly, which revived my exasperation with her, indeed a fierce desire never to let her go any more. I tightened my embrace in time, gasping out: "No— you don't!" as if she were my mortal enemy. On her part not a word was said. Putting her hands against my chest, she pushed with all her might without suc- ceeding to break the circle of my arms. Except that she seemed thoroughly awake now, her eyes gave me no clue whatever. To meet her black stare was like look- ing into a deep well, and I was totally unprepared for her change of tactics. Instead of trying to tear my hands apart, she flung herself upon my breast and with a downward, undulating, serpentine motion, a quick sliding dive, she got away from me smoothly. It was all very swift; I saw her pick up the tail of her wrapper and run for the door at the end of the verandah not very gracefully. She appeared to be limping a little—and then she vanished; the door swung behind her so noiselessly that I could not believe it was completely closed. I had a distinct suspicion of her black eye being at the crack to watch what I would do. I could not make up my mind whether to shake my fist in that direction or blow a kiss.

VI

EITHER would have been perfectly consistent with my feelings. I gazed at the door, hesitating, but in the end I did neither. The monition of some sixth sense—the sense of guilt, maybe, that sense which always acts too late, alas!—warned me to look round; and at once I became aware that the conclusion of this tumultuous episode was likely to be a matter of lively anxiety. Jacobus was standing in the doorway of the dining-room. How long he had been there it was impossible to guess; and remembering my struggle with the girl I thought he must have been its mute witness from beginning to end. But this supposition seemed almost incredible. Perhaps that impenetrable girl had heard him come in and had got away in time.

He stepped on to the verandah in his usual manner, heavy-eyed, with glued lips. I marvelled at the girl's resemblance to this man. Those long, Egyptian eyes, that low forehead of a stupid goddess, she had found in the sawdust of the circus; but all the rest of the face, the design and the modelling, the rounded chin, the very lips—all that was Jacobus, fined down, more finished, more expressive.

His thick hand fell on and grasped with force the back of a light chair (there were several standing about) and I perceived the chance of a broken head at the end of all this—most likely. My mortification was extreme. The scandal would be horrible; that was unavoidable. But how to act so as to satisfy myself I did not know. I stood on my guard and at any rate faced him. There was nothing else for it. Of one thing I was certain, that, however brazen my attitude, it could never equal the characteristic Jacobus impudence.

He gave me his melancholy, glued smile and sat down. I own I was relieved. The perspective of passing from kisses to blows had nothing particularly attractive in it. Perhaps—perhaps he had seen nothing? He behaved as usual, but he had never before found me alone on the verandah. If he had alluded to it, if he had asked: "Where's Alice?" or something of the sort, I would have been able to judge from the tone. He would give me no opportunity. The striking peculiarity was that he had never looked up at me yet. "He knows," I said to myself confidently. And my contempt for him relieved my disgust with myself.

"You are early home," I remarked.

"Things are very quiet; nothing doing at the store to-day," he explained with a cast-down air.

"Oh, well, you know, I am off," I said, feeling that this, perhaps, was the best thing to do.

"Yes," he breathed out. "Day after to-morrow."

This was not what I had meant; but as he gazed persistently on the floor, I followed the direction of his glance. In the absolute stillness of the house we stared at the high-heeled slipper the girl had lost in her flight. We stared. It lay overturned.

After what seemed a very long time to me, Jacobus hitched his chair forward, stooped with extended arm and picked it up. It looked a slender thing in his big, thick hands. It was not really a slipper, but a low shoe of blue, glazed kid, rubbed and shabby. It had straps to go over the instep, but the girl only thrust her feet in, after her slovenly manner. Jacobus raised his eyes from the shoe to look at me.

"Sit down, Captain," he said at last, in his subdued tone.

As if the sight of that shoe had renewed the spell, I gave up suddenly the idea of leaving the house there and then. It had become impossible. I sat down, keeping my eyes on the fascinating object. Jacobus turned his daughter's shoe over and over in his cushioned paws as if studying the way the thing was made. He contemplated the thin sole for a time; then glancing inside with an absorbed air:

"I am glad I found you here, Captain."

I answered this by some sort of grunt, watching him covertly. Then I added: "You won't have much more of me now."

He was still deep in the interior of that shoe on which my eyes too were resting.

"Have you thought any more of this deal in potatoes I spoke to you about the other day?"

"No, I haven't," I answered curtly. He checked my movement to rise by an austere, commanding gesture of the hand holding that fatal shoe. I remained seated and glared at him. "You know I don't trade."

"You ought to, Captain. You ought to."

I reflected. If I left that house now I would never see the girl again. And I felt I must see her once more, if only for an instant. It was a need, not to be reasoned with, not to be disregarded. No, I did not want to go away. I wanted to stay for one more experience of that strange provoking sensation and of indefinite desire, the habit of which had made me—me of all people!—dread the prospect of going to sea.

"Mr. Jacobus," I pronounced slowly. "Do you really think that upon the whole and taking various matters into consideration—I mean everything, do you understand?—it would be a good thing for me to trade, let us say, with you?"

I waited for a while. He went on looking at the shoe which he held now crushed in the middle, the worn point of the toe and the high heel protruding on each side of his heavy fist.

"That will be all right," he said, facing me squarely at last.

"Are you sure?"

"You'll find it quite correct, Captain." He had

uttered his habitual phrases in his usual placid, breath-saving voice and stood my hard, inquisitive stare sleepily without as much as a wink.

"Then let us trade," I said, turning my shoulder to him. "I see you are bent on it."

I did not want an open scandal, but I thought that outward decency may be bought too dearly at times. I included Jacobus, myself, the whole population of the island, in the same contemptuous disgust as though we had been partners in an ignoble transaction. And the remembered vision at sea, diaphanous and blue, of the Pearl of the Ocean at sixty miles off; the unsubstantial, clear marvel of it as if evoked by the art of a beautiful and pure magic, turned into a thing of horrors too. Was this the fortune this vaporous and rare apparition had held for me in its hard heart, hidden within the shape as of fair dreams and mist? Was this my luck?

"I think"—Jacobus became suddenly audible after what seemed the silence of vile meditation—"that you might conveniently take some thirty tons. That would be about the lot, Captain."

"Would it? The lot! I dare say it would be convenient, but I haven't got enough money for that."

I had never seen him so animated.

"No!" he exclaimed with what I took for the accent of grim menace. "That's a pity." He paused, then, unrelenting: "How much money have you got, Captain?" he inquired with awful directness.

It was my turn to face him squarely. I did so and mentioned the amount I could dispose of. And I perceived that he was disappointed. He thought it over, his calculating gaze lost in mine, for quite a long time before he came out in a thoughtful tone with the rapacious suggestion:

"You could draw some more from your charterers. That would be quite easy, Captain."

"No, I couldn't," I retorted brusquely. "I've drawn my salary up to date, and besides, the ship's accounts are closed."

I was growing furious. I pursued: "And I'll tell you what: if I could do it I wouldn't." Then throwing off all restraint, I added: "You are a bit too much of a Jacobus, Mr. Jacobus."

The tone alone was insulting enough, but he remained tranquil, only a little puzzled, till something seemed to dawn upon him; but the unwonted light in his eyes died out instantly. As a Jacobus on his native heath, what a mere skipper chose to say could not touch him, outcast as he was. As a ship-chandler he could stand anything. All I caught of his mumble was a vague— "quite correct," than which nothing could have been more egregiously false at bottom—to my view, at least. But I remembered—I had never forgotten—that I must see the girl. I did not mean to go. I meant to stay in the house till I had seen her once more.

"Look here!" I said finally. "I'll tell you what I'll do. I'll take as many of your confounded potatoes as my money will buy, on condition that you go off at once down to the wharf to see them loaded in the lighter and sent alongside the ship straight away. Take the invoice and a signed receipt with you. Here's the key of my desk. Give it to Burns. He will pay you."

He got up from his chair before I had finished speaking, but he refused to take the key. Burns would never do it. He wouldn't like to ask him even.

"Well, then," I said, eyeing him slightingly, "there's nothing for it, Mr. Jacobus, but you must wait on board till I come off to settle with you."

"That will be all right, Captain. I will go at once."

He seemed at a loss what to do with the girl's shoe he was still holding in his fist. Finally, looking dully at me, he put it down on the chair from which he had risen.

"And you, Captain? Won't you come along, too, just to see——"

"Don't bother about me. I'll take care of myself."

He remained perplexed for a moment, as if trying to understand; and then his weighty: "Certainly, certainly, Captain," seemed to be the outcome of some sudden thought. His big chest heaved. Was it a sigh? As he went out to hurry off those potatoes he never looked back at me.

I waited till the noise of his footsteps had died out of the dining-room, and I waited a little longer. Then turning towards the distant door I raised my voice along the verandah:

"Alice!"

Nothing answered me, not even a stir behind the door. Jacobus's house might have been made empty for me to make myself at home in. I did not call again. I had become aware of a great discouragement. I was mentally jaded, morally dejected. I turned to the garden again, sitting down with my elbows spread on the low balustrade, and took my head in my hands.

The evening closed upon me. The shadows lengthened, deepened, mingled together into a pool of twilight in which the flower-beds glowed like coloured embers; whiffs of heavy scent came to me as if the dusk of this hemisphere were but the dimness of a temple and the garden an enormous censer swinging before the altar of the stars. The colours of the blossoms deepened, losing their glow one by one.

The girl, when I turned my head at a slight noise,

appeared to me very tall and slender, advancing with a swaying limp, a floating and uneven motion which ended in the sinking of her shadowy form into the deep low chair. And I don't know why or whence I received the impression that she had come too late. She ought to have appeared at my call. She ought to have . . . It was as if a supreme opportunity had been missed.

I rose and took a seat close to her, nearly opposite her arm-chair. Her ever discontented voice addressed me at once, contemptuously:

"You are still here."

I pitched mine low.

"You have come out at last."

"I came to look for my shoe—before they bring in the lights."

It was her harsh, enticing whisper, subdued, not very steady, but its low tremulousness gave me no thrill now. I could only make out the oval of her face, her uncovered throat, the long, white gleam of her eyes. She was mysterious enough. Her hands were resting on the arms of the chair. But where was the mysterious and provoking sensation which was like the perfume of her flower-like youth? I said quietly:

"I have got your shoe here." She made no sound and I continued: "You had better give me your foot and I will put it on for you."

She made no movement. I bent low down and groped for her foot under the flounces of the wrapper. She did not withdraw it and I put on the shoe, buttoning the instep-strap. It was an inanimate foot. I lowered it gently to the floor.

"If you buttoned the strap you would not be losing your shoe, Miss Don't Care," I said, trying to be playful without conviction. I felt more like wailing over the lost illusion of vague desire, over the sudden conviction that I would never find again near her the strange, half-evil, half-tender sensation which had given its acrid flavour to so many days, which had made her appear tragic and promising, pitiful and provoking. That was all over.

"Your father picked it up," I said, thinking she might just as well be told of the fact.

"I am not afraid of papa—by himself," she declared scornfully.

"Oh! It's only in conjunction with his disreputable associates, strangers, the 'riff-raff of Europe' as your charming aunt or great-aunt says—men like me, for instance—that you——"

"I am not afraid of you," she snapped out.

"That's because you don't know that I am now doing business with your father. Yes, I am in fact doing exactly what he wants me to do. I've broken my promise to you. That's the sort of man I am. And now—aren't you afraid? If you believe what that dear, kind, truthful old lady says you ought to be."

It was with unexpected modulated softness that she affirmed:

"No. I am not afraid." She hesitated. . . . "Not now."

"Quite right. You needn't be. I shall not see you again before I go to sea." I rose and stood near her chair. "But I shall often think of you in this old garden, passing under the trees over there, walking between these gorgeous flower-beds. You must love this garden——"

"I love nothing."

I heard in her sullen tone the faint echo of that resentfully tragic note which I had found once so provoking. But it left me unmoved except for a sudden and weary conviction of the emptiness of all things under Heaven.

"Good-bye, Alice," I said.

She did not answer, she did not move. To merely take her hand, shake it, and go away seemed impossible, almost improper. I stooped without haste and pressed my lips to her smooth forehead. This was the moment when I realised clearly with a sort of terror my complete detachment from that unfortunate creature. And as I lingered in that cruel self-knowledge I felt the light touch of her arms falling languidly on my neck and received a hasty, awkward, haphazard kiss which missed my lips. No! She was not afraid; but I was no longer moved. Her arms slipped off my neck slowly, she made no sound, the deep wicker arm-chair creaked slightly; only a sense of my dignity prevented me fleeing headlong from that catastrophic revelation.

I traversed the dining-room slowly. I thought: She's listening to my footsteps; she can't help it; she'll hear me open and shut that door. And I closed it as gently behind me as if I had been a thief retreating with his ill-gotten booty. During that stealthy act I experienced the last touch of emotion in that house, at the thought of the girl I had left sitting there in the obscurity, with her heavy hair and empty eyes as black as the night itself, staring into the walled garden, silent, warm, odorous with the perfume of imprisoned flowers, which, like herself, were lost to sight in a world buried in darkness.

The narrow, ill-lighted, rustic streets I knew so well on my way to the harbour were extremely quiet. I felt in my heart that the further one ventures the better one understands how everything in our life is common, short, and empty; that it is in seeking the unknown in our sensations that we discover how mediocre are our

attempts and how soon defeated! Jacobus's boatman
was waiting at the steps with an unusual air of readiness.
He put me alongside the ship, but did not give me his
confidential "Good-evening, sah," and, instead of shov-
ing off at once, remained holding by the ladder.

I was a thousand miles from commercial affairs, when
on the dark quarter-deck Mr. Burns positively rushed
at me, stammering with excitement. He had been
pacing the deck distractedly for hours awaiting my
arrival. Just before sunset a lighter loaded with potatoes had come alongside with that fat ship-chandler himself sitting on the pile of sacks. He was now stuck immovable in the cabin. What was the meaning of it
all? Surely I did not——

"Yes, Mr. Burns, I did," I cut him short. He was
beginning to make gestures of despair when I stopped
that, too, by giving him the key of my desk and desiring
him, in a tone which admitted of no argument, to go
below at once, pay Mr. Jacobus's bill, and send him
out of the ship.

"I don't want to see him," I confessed frankly,
climbing the poop-ladder. I felt extremely tired.
Dropping on the seat of the skylight, I gave myself up
to idle gazing at the lights about the quay and at the
black mass of the mountain on the south side of the
harbour. I never heard Jacobus leave the ship with
every single sovereign of my ready cash in his pocket.
I never heard anything till, a long time afterwards, Mr.
Burns, unable to contain himself any longer, intruded
upon me with his ridiculously angry lamentations at
my weakness and good nature.

"Of course, there's plenty of room in the after-hatch.
But they are sure to go rotten down there. Well! I
never heard . . . seventeen tons! I suppose I
must hoist in that lot first thing to-morrow morning."

"I suppose you must. Unless you drop them over-board. But I'm afraid you can't do that. I wouldn't mind myself, but it's forbidden to throw rubbish into the harbour, you know."

"That is the truest word you have said for many a day, sir—rubbish. That's just what I expect they are. Nearly eighty good gold sovereigns gone; a perfectly clean sweep of your drawer, sir. Bless me if I understand!"

As it was impossible to throw the right light on this commercial transaction I left him to his lamentations and under the impression that I was a hopeless fool. Next day I did not go ashore. For one thing, I had no money to go ashore with—no, not enough to buy a cigarette. Jacobus had made a clean sweep. But that was not the only reason. The Pearl of the Ocean had in a few short hours grown odious to me. And I did not want to meet any one. My reputation had suffered. I knew I was the object of unkind and sarcastic comments.

The following morning at sunrise, just as our stern-fasts had been let go and the tug plucked us out from between the buoys, I saw Jacobus standing up in his boat. The nigger was pulling hard; several baskets of provisions for ships were stowed between the thwarts. The father of Alice was going his morning round. His countenance was tranquil and friendly. He raised his arm and shouted something with great heartiness. But his voice was of the sort that doesn't carry any distance; all I could catch faintly, or rather guess at, were the words "next time" and "quite correct." And it was only of these last that I was certain. Raising my arm perfunctorily for all response, I turned away. I rather resented the familiarity of the thing. Hadn't I settled accounts finally with him by means of that potato bargain?

This being a harbour story it is not my purpose to
speak of our passage. I was glad enough to be at sea,
but not with the gladness of old days. Formerly I had
no memories to take away with me. I shared in the
blessed forgetfulness of sailors, that forgetfulness
natural and invincible, which resembles innocence in
so far that it prevents self-examination. Now however I remembered the girl. During the first few days
I was for ever questioning myself as to the nature of
facts and sensations connected with her person and
with my conduct.

And I must say also that Mr. Burns' intolerable
fussing with those potatoes was not calculated to make
me forget the part which I had played. He looked
upon it as a purely commercial transaction of a particularly foolish kind, and his devotion—if it was
devotion and not mere cussedness as I came to regard
it before long—inspired him with a zeal to minimise
my loss as much as possible. Oh, yes! He took care
of those infamous potatoes with a vengeance, as the
saying goes.

Everlastingly, there was a tackle over the after-hatch
and everlastingly the watch on deck were pulling up,
spreading out, picking over, rebagging, and lowering
down again, some part of that lot of potatoes. My
bargain with all its remotest associations, mental and
visual—the garden of flowers and scents, the girl with
her provoking contempt and her tragic loneliness of a
hopeless castaway—was everlastingly dangled before
my eyes, for thousands of miles along the open sea.
And as if by a satanic refinement of irony it was accompanied by a most awful smell. Whiffs from decaying
potatoes pursued me on the poop, they mingled with
my thoughts, with my food, poisoned my very dreams.
They made an atmosphere of corruption for the ship.

I remonstrated with Mr. Burns about this excessive care. I would have been well content to batten the hatch down and let them perish under the deck.

That perhaps would have been unsafe. The horrid emanations might have flavoured the cargo of sugar. They seemed strong enough to taint the very ironwork. In addition Mr. Burns made it a personal matter. He assured me he knew how to treat a cargo of potatoes at sea—had been in the trade as a boy, he said. He meant to make my loss as small as possible. What between his devotion—it must have been devotion—and his vanity, I positively dared not give him the order to throw my commercial venture overboard. I believe he would have refused point blank to obey my lawful command. An unprecedented and comical situation would have been created with which I did not feel equal to deal.

I welcomed the coming of bad weather as no sailor had ever done. When at last I hove the ship to, to pick up the pilot outside Port Philip Heads, the after-hatch had not been opened for more than a week and I might have believed that no such thing as a potato had ever been on board.

It was an abominable day, raw, blustering, with great squalls of wind and rain; the pilot, a cheery person, looked after the ship and chatted to me, streaming from head to foot; and the heavier the lash of the downpour the more pleased with himself and everything around him he seemed to be. He rubbed his wet hands with a satisfaction, which to me, who had stood that kind of thing for several days and nights, seemed inconceivable in any non-aquatic creature.

"You seem to enjoy getting wet, Pilot," I remarked.

He had a bit of land round his house in the suburbs and it was of his garden he was thinking. At the sound of the word garden, unheard, unspoken for so many days, I had a vision of gorgeous colour, of sweet scents, of a girlish figure crouching in a chair. Yes. That was a distinct emotion breaking into the peace I had found in the sleepless anxieties of my responsibility during a week of dangerous bad weather. The Colony, the pilot explained, had suffered from unparalleled drought. This was the first decent drop of water they had had for seven months. The root crops were lost. And, trying to be casual, but with visible interest, he asked me if I had perchance any potatoes to spare.

Potatoes! I had managed to forget them. In a moment I felt plunged into corruption up to my neck. Mr. Burns was making eyes at me behind the pilot's back.

Finally, he obtained a ton, and paid ten pounds for it. This was twice the price of my bargain with Jacobus. The spirit of covetousness woke up in me. That night, in harbour, before I slept, the Custom House galley came alongside. While his underlings were putting seals on the store-rooms, the officer in charge took me aside confidentially. "I say, Captain, you don't happen to have any potatoes to sell?"

Clearly there was a potato famine in the land. I let him have a ton for twelve pounds and he went away joyfully. That night I dreamt of a pile of gold in the form of a grave in which a girl was buried, and woke up callous with greed. On calling at my ship-broker's office, that man, after the usual business had been transacted, pushed his spectacles up on his forehead.

"I was thinking, Captain, that coming from the Pearl of the Ocean you may have some potatoes to sell."

I said negligently: "Oh, yes, I could spare you a ton. Fifteen pounds."

He exclaimed: "I say!" But after studying my face for a while accepted my terms with a faint grimace. It seems that these people could not exist without potatoes. I could. I didn't want to see a potato as long as I lived; but the demon of lucre had taken possession of me. How the news got about I don't know, but, returning on board rather late, I found a small group of men of the coster type hanging about the waist, while Mr. Burns walked to and fro the quarter-deck loftily, keeping a triumphant eye on them. They had come to buy potatoes.

"These chaps have been waiting here in the sun for hours," Burns whispered to me excitedly. "They have drunk the water-cask dry. Don't you throw away your chances, sir. You are too good-natured."

I selected a man with thick legs and a man with a cast in his eye to negotiate with; simply because they were easily distinguishable from the rest. "You have the money on you?" I inquired, before taking them down into the cabin.

"Yes, sir," they answered in one voice, slapping their pockets. I liked their air of quiet determination. Long before the end of the day all the potatoes were sold at about three times the price I had paid for them. Mr. Burns, feverish and exulting, congratulated himself on his skilful care of my commercial venture, but hinted plainly that I ought to have made more of it.

That night I did not sleep very well. I thought of Jacobus by fits and starts, between snatches of dreams concerned with castaways starving on a desert island covered with flowers. It was extremely unpleasant. In the morning, tired and unrefreshed, I sat down and wrote a long letter to my owners, giving them a carefully-thought-out scheme for the ship's employment in the East and about the China Seas for the next two years. I spent the day at that task and felt somewhat more at peace when it was done.

Their reply came in due course. They were greatly struck with my project; but considering that, notwithstanding the unfortunate difficulty with the bags (which they trusted I would know how to guard against in the future), the voyage showed a very fair profit, they thought it would be better to keep the ship in the sugar trade—at least for the present.

I turned over the page and read on:

"We have had a letter from our good friend Mr. Jacobus. We are pleased to see how well you have hit it off with him; for, not to speak of his assistance in the unfortunate matter of the bags, he writes us that should you, by using all possible dispatch, manage to bring the ship back early in the season he would be able to give us a good rate of freight. We have no doubt that your best endeavours . . . etc. . . . etc."

I dropped the letter and sat motionless for a long time. Then I wrote my answer (it was a short one) and went ashore myself to post it. But I passed one letter-box, then another, and in the end found myself going up Collins Street with the letter still in my pocket—against my heart. Collins Street at four o'clock in the afternoon is not exactly a desert solitude; but I had never felt more isolated from the rest of mankind than when I walked that day its crowded pavement, battling desperately with my thoughts and feeling already vanquished.

There came a moment when the awful tenacity of Jacobus, the man of one passion and of one idea, appeared to me almost heroic. He had not given me up. He had gone again to his odious brother. And then he appeared to me odious himself. Was it for his own sake or for the sake of the poor girl? And on that last supposition the memory of the kiss which missed my lips appalled me; for whatever he had seen, or guessed at, or risked, he knew nothing of that. Unless the girl had told him. How could I go back to fan that fatal spark with my cold breath? No, no, that unexpected kiss had to be paid for at its full price.

At the first letter-box I came to I stopped and reaching into my breast-pocket I took out the letter—it was as if I were plucking out my very heart—and dropped it through the slit. Then I went straight on board.

I wondered what dreams I would have that night; but as it turned out I did not sleep at all. At breakfast I informed Mr. Burns that I had resigned my command.

He dropped his knife and fork and looked at me with indignation.

"You have, sir! I thought you loved the ship."

"So I do, Burns," I said. "But the fact is that the Indian Ocean and everything that is in it has lost its charm for me. I am going home as passenger by the Suez Canal."

"Everything that is in it," he repeated angrily. "I've never heard anybody talk like this. And to tell you the truth, sir, all the time we have been together I've never quite made you out. What's one ocean more than another? Charm, indeed!"

He was really devoted to me, I believe. But he cheered up when I told him that I had recommended him for my successor.

"Anyhow," he remarked, "let people say what they like, this Jacobus has served your turn. I must admit that this potato business has paid extremely well. Of course, if only you had——"

"Yes, Mr. Burns," I interrupted. "Quite a smile of fortune."

But I could not tell him that it was driving me out of the ship I had learned to love. And as I sat heavy-hearted at that parting, seeing all my plans destroyed, my modest future endangered—for this command was like a foot in the stirrup for a young man—he gave up completely for the first time his critical attitude.

"A wonderful piece of luck!" he said.

THE SECRET SHARER

AN EPISODE FROM THE COAST

THE SECRET SHARER

I

On my right hand there were lines of fishing-stakes resembling a mysterious system of half-submerged bamboo fences, incomprehensible in its division of the domain of tropical fishes, and crazy of aspect as if abandoned for ever by some nomad tribe of fishermen now gone to the other end of the ocean; for there was no sign of human habitation as far as the eye could reach. To the left a group of barren islets, suggesting ruins of stone walls, towers, and blockhouses, had its foundations set in a blue sea that itself looked solid, so still and stable did it lie below my feet; even the track of light from the westering sun shone smoothly, without that animated glitter which tells of an imperceptible ripple. And when I turned my head to take a parting glance at the tug which had just left us anchored outside the bar, I saw the straight line of the flat shore joined to the stable sea, edge to edge, with a perfect and unmarked closeness, in one levelled floor half brown, half blue under the enormous dome of the sky. Corresponding in their insignificance to the islets of the sea, two small clumps of trees, one on each side of the only fault in the impeccable joint, marked the mouth of the river Meinam we had just left on the first preparatory stage of our homeward journey; and, far back on the inland level, a larger and loftier mass, the grove surrounding the great Paknam pagoda, was the only thing on which the eye could rest from the vain task of ex-

ploring the monotonous sweep of the horizon. Here
and there gleams as of a few scattered pieces of silver
marked the windings of the great river; and on the
nearest of them, just within the bar, the tug steaming
right into the land became lost to my sight, hull and
funnel and masts, as though the impassive earth had
swallowed her up without an effort, without a tremor.
My eye followed the light cloud of her smoke, now here,
now there, above the plain, according to the devious
curves of the stream, but always fainter and farther
away, till I lost it at last behind the mitre-shaped hill
of the great pagoda. And then I was left alone with
my ship, anchored at the head of the Gulf of Siam.

She floated at the starting-point of a long journey,
very still in an immense stillness, the shadows of her
spars flung far to the eastward by the setting sun. At
that moment I was alone on her decks. There was
not a sound in her—and around us nothing moved,
nothing lived, not a canoe on the water, not a bird in
the air, not a cloud in the sky. In this breathless
pause at the threshold of a long passage we seemed to
be measuring our fitness for a long and arduous enterprise, the appointed task of both our existences to be
carried out, far from all human eyes, with only sky and
sea for spectators and for judges.

There must have been some glare in the air to interfere with one's sight, because it was only just before the
sun left us that my roaming eyes made out beyond the
highest ridge of the principal islet of the group something which did away with the solemnity of perfect
solitude. The tide of darkness flowed on swiftly; and
with tropical suddenness a swarm of stars came out
above the shadowy earth, while I lingered yet, my hand
resting lightly on my ship's rail as if on the shoulder of
a trusted friend. But, with all that multitude of

celestial bodies staring down at one, the comfort of quiet communion with her was gone for good. And there were also disturbing sounds by this time—voices, footsteps forward; the steward flitted along the main-deck, a busily ministering spirit; a hand-bell tinkled urgently under the poop-deck. . . .

I found my two officers waiting for me near the supper table, in the lighted cuddy. We sat down at once, and as I helped the chief mate, I said:

"Are you aware that there is a ship anchored inside the islands? I saw her mastheads above the ridge as the sun went down."

He raised sharply his simple face, overcharged by a terrible growth of whisker, and emitted his usual ejaculations: "Bless my soul, sir! You don't say so!"

My second mate was a round-cheeked, silent young man, grave beyond his years, I thought; but as our eyes happened to meet I detected a slight quiver on his lips. I looked down at once. It was not my part to en-courage sneering on board my ship. It must be said, too, that I knew very little of my officers. In con-sequence of certain events of no particular significance, except to myself, I had been appointed to the command only a fortnight before. Neither did I know much of the hands forward. All these people had been together for eighteen months or so, and my position was that of the only stranger on board. I mention this because it has some bearing on what is to follow. But what I felt most was my being a stranger to the ship; and if all the truth must be told, I was somewhat of a stranger to myself. The youngest man on board (barring the second mate), and untried as yet by a position of the fullest responsibility, I was willing to take the adequacy of the others for granted. They had simply to be equal to their tasks; but I wondered how far I should turn out faithful to that ideal conception of one's own personality every man sets up for himself secretly.

Meantime the chief mate, with an almost visible effect of collaboration on the part of his round eyes and frightful whiskers, was trying to evolve a theory of the anchored ship. His dominant trait was to take all things into earnest consideration. He was of a painstaking turn of mind. As he used to say, he "liked to account to himself" for practically everything that came in his way, down to a miserable scorpion he had found in his cabin a week before. The why and the wherefore of that scorpion—how it got on board and came to select his room rather than the pantry (which was a dark place and more what a scorpion would be partial to), and how on earth it managed to drown itself in the inkwell of his writing-desk—had exercised him infinitely. The ship within the islands was much more easily accounted for; and just as we were about to rise from table he made his pronouncement. She was, he doubted not, a ship from home lately arrived. Probably she drew too much water to cross the bar except at the top of spring tides. Therefore she went into that natural harbour to wait for a few days in preference to remaining in an open roadstead.

"That's so," confirmed the second mate, suddenly, in his slightly hoarse voice. "She draws over twenty feet. She's the Liverpool ship *Sephora* with a cargo of coal. Hundred and twenty-three days from Cardiff."

We looked at him in surprise.

"The tugboat skipper told me when he came on board for your letters, sir," explained the young man. "He expects to take her up the river the day after to-morrow."

After thus overwhelming us with the extent of his information he slipped out of the cabin. The mate observed regretfully that he "could not account for that young fellow's whims." What prevented him telling us all about it at once, he wanted to know.

I detained him as he was making a move. For the last two days the crew had had plenty of hard work, and the night before they had very little sleep. I felt painfully that I—a stranger—was doing something unusual when I directed him to let all hands turn in without setting an anchor-watch. I proposed to keep on deck myself till one o'clock or thereabouts. I would get the second mate to relieve me at that hour.

"He will turn out the cook and the steward at four," I concluded, "and then give you a call. Of course at the slightest sign of any sort of wind we'll have the hands up and make a start at once."

He concealed his astonishment. "Very well, sir." Outside the cuddy he put his head in the second mate's door to inform him of my unheard-of caprice to take a five hours' anchor-watch on myself. I heard the other raise his voice incredulously—"What? The Captain himself?" Then a few more murmurs, a door closed, then another. A few moments later I went on deck.

My strangeness, which had made me sleepless, had prompted that unconventional arrangement, as if I had expected in those solitary hours of the night to get on terms with the ship of which I knew nothing, manned by men of whom I knew very little more. Fast alongside a wharf, littered like any ship in port with a tangle of unrelated things, invaded by unrelated shore people, I had hardly seen her yet properly. Now, as she lay cleared for sea, the stretch of her main-deck seemed to me very fine under the stars. Very fine, very roomy for her size, and very inviting. I descended the poop and paced the waist, my mind picturing to myself the coming passage through the Malay Archipelago, down the Indian Ocean, and up the Atlantic. All its phases were familiar enough to me, every characteristic, all the alternatives which were likely to face me on the high seas—everything! . . . except the novel responsibility of command. But I took heart from the reasonable thought that the ship was like other ships, the men like other men, and that the sea was not likely to keep any special surprises expressly for my discomfiture.

Arrived at that comforting conclusion, I bethought myself of a cigar and went below to get it. All was still down there. Everybody at the after end of the ship was sleeping profoundly. I came out again on the quarter-deck, agreeably at ease in my sleeping-suit on that warm breathless night, barefooted, a glowing cigar in my teeth, and, going forward, I was met by the profound silence of the fore end of the ship. Only as I passed the door of the forecastle I heard a deep, quiet, trustful sigh of some sleeper inside. And suddenly I rejoiced in the great security of the sea as compared with the unrest of the land, in my choice of that untempted life presenting no disquieting problems, invested with an elementary moral beauty by the absolute straightforwardness of its appeal and by the singleness of its purpose.

The riding-light in the fore-rigging burned with a clear, untroubled, as if symbolic, flame, confident and bright in the mysterious shades of the night. Passing on my way aft along the other side of the ship, I observed that the rope side-ladder, put over, no doubt, for the master of the tug when he came to fetch away our letters, had not been hauled in as it should have been. I became annoyed at this, for exactitude in small matters is the very soul of discipline. Then I reflected that I had myself peremptorily dismissed my officers from duty, and by my own act had prevented the anchor-watch being formally set and things properly attended to. I asked myself whether it was wise ever to interfere with the established routine of duties even from the kindest of motives. My action might have made me appear eccentric. Goodness only knew how that absurdly whiskered mate would "account" for my conduct, and what the whole ship thought of that informality of their new captain. I was vexed with myself.

Not from compunction certainly, but, as it were mechanically, I proceeded to get the ladder in myself. Now a side-ladder of that sort is a light affair and comes in easily, yet my vigorous tug, which should have brought it flying on board, merely recoiled upon my body in a totally unexpected jerk. What the devil! . . . I was so astounded by the immovableness of that ladder that I remained stock-still, trying to account for it to myself like that imbecile mate of mine. In the end, of course, I put my head over the rail.

The side of the ship made an opaque belt of shadow on the darkling glassy shimmer of the sea. But I saw at once something elongated and pale floating very close to the ladder. Before I could form a guess a faint flash of phosphorescent light, which seemed to issue suddenly from the naked body of a man, flickered in the sleeping water with the elusive, silent play of summer lightning in a night sky. With a gasp I saw revealed to my stare a pair of feet, the long legs, a broad livid back immersed right up to the neck in a greenish cadaverous glow. One hand, awash, clutched the bottom rung of the ladder. He was complete but for the head. A headless corpse! The cigar dropped out of my gaping mouth with a tiny plop and a short hiss quite audible in the absolute stillness of all things under heaven. At that I suppose he raised up his face, a dimly pale oval in the shadow of the ship's side. But even then I could only barely make out down there the shape of his black-haired head. However, it was enough for the horrid, frost-bound sensation which had gripped me about the chest to pass off. The moment of vain exclamations was past, too. I only climbed on the spare spar and leaned over the rail as far as I could, to bring my eyes nearer to that mystery floating alongside.

As he hung by the ladder, like a resting swimmer, the sea-lightning played about his limbs at every stir; and he appeared in it ghastly, silvery, fish-like. He remained as mute as a fish, too. He made no motion to get out of the water, either. It was inconceivable that he should not attempt to come on board, and strangely troubling to suspect that perhaps he did not want to. And my first words were prompted by just that troubled incertitude.

"What's the matter?" I asked in my ordinary tone, speaking down to the face upturned exactly under mine.

"Cramp," it answered, no louder. Then slightly anxious, "I say, no need to call any one."

"I was not going to," I said.

"Are you alone on deck?"

"Yes."

I had somehow the impression that he was on the point of letting go the ladder to swim away beyond my ken—mysterious as he came. But, for the moment, this being appearing as if he had risen from the bottom of the sea (it was certainly the nearest land to the ship) wanted only to know the time. I told him. And he, down there, tentatively:

"I suppose your captain's turned in?"

"I am sure he isn't," I said.

He seemed to struggle with himself, for I heard something like the low, bitter murmur of doubt. "What's the good?" His next words came out with a hesitating effort.

"Look here, my man. Could you call him out quietly?"

I thought the time had come to declare myself.

"*I* am the captain."

I heard a "By Jove!" whispered at the level of the water. The phosphorescence flashed in the swirl of the water all about his limbs, his other hand seized the ladder.

"My name's Leggatt."

The voice was calm and resolute. A good voice. The self-possession of that man had somehow induced a corresponding state in myself. It was very quietly that I remarked:

"You must be a good swimmer."

"Yes. I've been in the water practically since nine o'clock. The question for me now is whether I am to let go this ladder and go on swimming till I sink from exhaustion, or—to come on board here."

I felt this was no mere formula of desperate speech, but a real alternative in the view of a strong soul. I should have gathered from this that he was young; indeed, it is only the young who are ever confronted by such clear issues. But at the time it was pure intuition on my part. A mysterious communication was established already between us two—in the face of that silent, darkened tropical sea. I was young, too; young enough to make no comment. The man in the water began suddenly to climb up the ladder, and I hastened away from the rail to fetch some clothes.

Before entering the cabin I stood still, listening in the lobby at the foot of the stairs. A faint snore came through the closed door of the chief mate's room. The second mate's door was on the hook, but the darkness in there was absolutely soundless. He, too, was young and could sleep like a stone. Remained the steward, but he was not likely to wake up before he was called. I got a sleeping-suit out of my room and, coming back on deck, saw the naked man from the sea sitting on the main-hatch, glimmering white in the darkness. his elbows on his knees and his head in his hands. In a moment he had concealed his damp body in a sleeping-suit of the same grey-stripe pattern as the one I was wearing and followed me like my double on the poop. Together we moved right aft, barefooted, silent.

"What is it?" I asked in a deadened voice, taking the lighted lamp out of the binnacle, and raising it to his face.

"An ugly business."

He had rather regular features; a good mouth; light eyes under somewhat heavy, dark eyebrows; a smooth, square forehead; no growth on his cheeks; a small, brown moustache, and a well-shaped, round chin. His expression was concentrated, meditative, under the inspecting light of the lamp I held up to his face; such as a man thinking hard in solitude might wear. My sleeping-suit was just right for his size. A well-knit young fellow of twenty-five at most. He caught his lower lip with the edge of white, even teeth.

"Yes," I said, replacing the lamp in the binnacle. The warm, heavy tropical night closed upon his head again.

"There's a ship over there," he murmured.

"Yes, I know. The *Sephora*. Did you know of us?"

"Hadn't the slightest idea. I am the mate of her——" He paused and corrected himself. "I should say I *was*."

"Aha! Something wrong?"

"Yes. Very wrong indeed. I've killed a man."

"What do you mean? Just now?"

"No, on the passage. Weeks ago. Thirty-nine south. When I say a man——"

"Fit of temper," I suggested, confidently.

The shadowy, dark head, like mine, seemed to nod imperceptibly above the ghostly grey of my sleeping-suit. It was, in the night, as though I had been faced by my own reflection in the depths of a sombre and immense mirror.

"A pretty thing to have to own up to for a Conway boy," murmured my double, distinctly.

"You're a Conway boy?"

"I am," he said, as if startled. Then, slowly . . . "Perhaps you too——"

It was so; but being a couple of years older I had left before he joined. After a quick interchange of dates a silence fell; and I thought suddenly of my absurd mate with his terrific whiskers and the "Bless my soul—you don't say so" type of intellect. My double gave me an inkling of his thoughts by saying: "My father's a parson in Norfolk. Do you see me before a judge and jury on that charge? For myself I can't see the necessity. There are fellows that an angel from heaven—— And I am not that. He was one of those creatures that are just simmering all the time with a silly sort of wickedness. Miserable devils that have no business to live at all. He wouldn't do his duty and wouldn't let anybody else do theirs. But what's the good of talking! You know well enough the sort of ill-conditioned snarling cur——"

He appealed to me as if our experiences had been as identical as our clothes. And I knew well enough the pestiferous danger of such a character where there are no means of legal repression. And I knew well enough also that my double there was no homicidal ruffian. I did not think of asking him for details, and he told me the story roughly in brusque, disconnected sentences. I needed no more. I saw it all going on as though I were myself inside that other sleeping-suit.

"It happened while we were setting a reefed fore-sail, at dusk. Reefed foresail! You understand the sort of weather. The only sail we had left to keep the ship running; so you may guess what it had been like for days. Anxious sort of job, that. He gave me some of his cursed insolence at the sheet. I tell you I was overdone with this terrific weather that seemed to have no end to it. Terrific, I tell you—and a deep ship. I believe the fellow himself was half crazed with funk. It was no time for gentlemanly reproof, so I turned round and felled him like an ox. He up and at me. We closed just as an awful sea made for the ship. All hands saw it coming and took to the rigging, but I had him by the throat, and went on shaking him like a rat, the men above us yelling, 'Look out! look out!'" Then a crash as if the sky had fallen on my head. They say that for over ten minutes hardly any-thing was to be seen of the ship—just the three masts and a bit of the forecastle head and of the poop all awash driving along in a smother of foam. It was a miracle that they found us, jammed together behind the forebits. It's clear that I meant business, be-cause I was holding him by the throat still when they picked us up. He was black in the face. It was too much for them. It seems they rushed us aft together, gripped as we were, screaming 'Murder!' like a lot of lunatics, and broke into the cuddy. And the ship running for her life, touch and go all the time, any minute her last in a sea fit to turn your hair grey only a-looking at it. I understand that the skipper, too, started raving like the rest of them. The man had been deprived of sleep for more than a week, and to have this sprung on him at the height of a furious gale nearly drove him out of his mind. I wonder they didn't fling me overboard after getting the carcass of their precious ship-mate out of my fingers. They had rather a job to separate us, I've been told. A sufficiently fierce story to make an old judge and a respectable jury sit up a bit. The first thing I heard when I came to myself was the maddening howling of that endless gale, and on that the voice of the old man. He was hanging on to my bunk, staring into my face out of his sou'wester.

"'Mr. Leggatt, you have killed a man. You can act no longer as chief mate of this ship.'"

His care to subdue his voice made it sound monotonous. He rested a hand on the end of the skylight to steady himself with, and all that time did not stir a limb, so far as I could see. "Nice little tale for a quiet tea-party," he concluded in the same tone.

One of my hands, too, rested on the end of the skylight; neither did I stir a limb, so far as I knew. We stood less than a foot from each other. It occurred to me that if old "Bless my soul—you don't say so" were to put his head up the companion and catch sight of us, he would think he was seeing double, or imagine himself come upon a scene of weird witchcraft; the strange captain having a quiet confabulation by the wheel with his own grey ghost. I became very much concerned to prevent anything of the sort. I heard the other's soothing undertone.

"My father's a parson in Norfolk," it said. Evidently

he had forgotten he had told me this important fact before. Truly a nice little tale.

"You had better slip down into my stateroom now," I said, moving off stealthily. My double followed my movements; our bare feet made no sound; I let him in, closed the door with care, and, after giving a call to the second mate, returned on deck for my relief.

"Not much sign of any wind yet," I remarked when he approached.

"No, sir. Not much," he assented, sleepily, in his hoarse voice, with just enough deference, no more, and barely suppressing a yawn.

"Well, that's all you have to look out for. You have got your orders."

"Yes, sir."

I paced a turn or two on the poop and saw him take up his position face forward with his elbow in the ratlines of the mizzen-rigging before I went below. The mate's faint snoring was still going on peacefully. The cuddy lamp was burning over the table on which stood a vase with flowers, a polite attention from the ship's provision merchant—the last flowers we should see for the next three months at the very least. Two bunches of bananas hung from the beam symmetrically, one on each side of the rudder-casing. Everything was as before in the ship—except that two of her captain's sleeping-suits were simultaneously in use, one motionless in the cuddy, the other keeping very still in the captain's stateroom.

It must be explained here that my cabin had the form of the capital letter L the door being within the angle and opening into the short part of the letter. A couch was to the left, the bed-place to the right; my writing-desk and the chronometers' table faced the door. But any one opening it, unless he stepped right inside, had no view of what I call the long (or vertical) part of the letter. It contained some lockers surmounted by a bookcase; and a few clothes, a thick jacket or two, caps, oilskin coat, and such like, hung on hooks. There was at the bottom of that part a door opening into my bath-room, which could be entered also directly from the saloon. But that way was never used.

The mysterious arrival had discovered the advantage of this particular shape. Entering my room, lighted strongly by a big bulkhead lamp swung on gimbals above my writing-desk, I did not see him anywhere till he stepped out quietly from behind the coats hung in the recessed part.

"I heard somebody moving about, and went in there at once," he whispered.

I, too, spoke under my breath.

"Nobody is likely to come in here without knocking and getting permission."

He nodded. His face was thin and the sunburn faded, as though he had been ill. And no wonder. He had been, I heard presently, kept under arrest in his cabin for nearly seven weeks. But there was nothing sickly in his eyes or in his expression. He was not a bit like me, really; yet, as we stood leaning over my bed-place, whispering side by side, with our dark heads together and our backs to the door, anybody bold enough to open it stealthily would have been treated to the uncanny sight of a double captain busy talking in whispers with his other self.

"But all this doesn't tell me how you came to hang on to our side-ladder," I inquired, in the hardly audible murmurs we used, after he had told me something more of the proceedings on board the *Sephora* once the bad weather was over.

"When we sighted Java Head I had had time to

think all those matters out several times over. I had six weeks of doing nothing else, and with only an hour or so every evening for a tramp on the quarter-deck."

He whispered, his arms folded on the side of my bed-place, staring through the open port. And I could imagine perfectly the manner of this thinking out—a stubborn if not a steadfast operation; something of which I should have been perfectly incapable.

"I reckoned it would be dark before we closed with the land," he continued, so low that I had to strain my hearing, near as we were to each other, shoulder touching shoulder almost. "So I asked to speak to the old man. He always seemed very sick when he came to see me—as if he could not look me in the face. You know, that foresail saved the ship. She was too deep to have run long under bare poles. And it was I that managed to set it for him. Anyway, he came. When I had him in my cabin—he stood by the door looking at me as if I had the halter round my neck already—I asked him right away to leave my cabin door unlocked at night while the ship was going through Sunda Straits. There would be the Java coast within two or three miles, off Angier Point. I wanted nothing more. I've had a prize for swimming my second year in the Conway."

"I can believe it," I breathed out.

"God only knows why they locked me in every night. To see some of their faces you'd have thought they were afraid I'd go about at night strangling people. Am I a murdering brute? Do I look it? By Jove! if I had been he wouldn't have trusted himself like that into my room. You'll say I might have chucked him aside and bolted out, there and then—it was dark already. Well, no. And for the same reason I wouldn't think of try-ing to smash the door. There would have been a rush to stop me at the noise, and I did not mean to get into a confounded scrimmage. Somebody else might have got killed—for I would not have broken out only to get chucked back, and I did not want any more of that work. He refused, looking more sick than ever. He was afraid of the men, and also of that old second mate of his who had been sailing with him for years—a grey-headed old humbug; and his steward, too, had been with him devil knows how long—seventeen years or more—a dogmatic sort of loafer who hated me like poison, just because I was the chief mate. No chief mate ever made more than one voyage in the *Sephora*, you know. Those two old chaps ran the ship. Devil only knows what the skipper wasn't afraid of (all his nerve went to pieces altogether in that hellish spell of bad weather we had)—of what the law would do to him—of his wife, perhaps. Oh, yes! she's on board. Though I don't think she would have meddled. She would have been only too glad to have me out of the ship in any way. The 'brand of Cain' business, don't you see. That's all right. I was ready enough to go off wandering on the face of the earth—and that was price enough to pay for an Abel of that sort. Anyhow, he wouldn't listen to me. 'This thing must take its course. I represent the law here.' He was shaking like a leaf. 'So you won't?' 'No!' 'Then I hope you will be able to sleep on that,' I said, and turned my back on him. 'I wonder that *you* can,' cries he, and locks the door.

"Well, after that, I couldn't. Not very well. That was three weeks ago. We have had a slow passage through the Java Sea; drifted about Carimata for ten days. When we anchored here they thought, I suppose, it was all right. The nearest land (and that's five miles) is the ship's destination; the consul would soon set about catching me; and there would have been

no object in bolting to these islets there. I don't
suppose there's a drop of water on them. I don't know
how it was, but to-night that steward, after bringing
me my supper, went out to let me eat it, and left the
door unlocked. And I ate it—all there was, too.
After I had finished I strolled out on the quarter-deck.
I don't know that I meant to do anything. A breath of
fresh air was all I wanted, I believe. Then a sudden
temptation came over me. I kicked off my slippers and
was in the water before I had made up my mind fairly.
Somebody heard the splash and they raised an awful
hullabaloo. 'He's gone! Lower the boats! He's committed suicide! No, he's swimming.' Certainly I was
swimming. It's not so easy for a swimmer like me to
commit suicide by drowning. I landed on the nearest
islet before the boat left the ship's side. I heard them
pulling about in the dark, hailing, and so on, but after a
bit they gave up. Everything quieted down and the
anchorage became as still as death. I sat down on a
stone and began to think. I felt certain they would
start searching for me at daylight. There was no place
to hide on those stony things—and if there had been,
what would have been the good? But now I was clear
of that ship, I was not going back. So after a while I
took off all my clothes, tied them up in a bundle with
a stone inside, and dropped them in the deep water on
the outer side of that islet. That was suicide enough
for me. Let them think what they liked, but I didn't
mean to drown myself. I meant to swim till I sank—
but that's not the same thing. I struck out for another
of these little islands, and it was from that one that I
first saw your riding-light. Something to swim for.
I went on easily, and on the way I came upon a flat
rock a foot or two above water. In the daytime, I
dare say, you might make it out with a glass from your

poop. I scrambled up on it and rested myself for a bit.
Then I made another start. That last spell must have
been over a mile."

His whisper was getting fainter and fainter, and all
the time he stared straight out through the port-hole,
in which there was not even a star to be seen. I had
not interrupted him. There was something that made
comment impossible in his narrative, or perhaps in
himself; a sort of feeling, a quality, which I can't find
a name for. And when he ceased, all I found was a
futile whisper: "So you swam for our light?"

"Yes—straight for it. It was something to swim
for. I couldn't see any stars low down because the
coast was in the way, and I couldn't see the land, either.
The water was like glass. One might have been swimming in a confounded thousand-feet deep cistern with
no place for scrambling out anywhere; but what I didn't
like was the notion of swimming round and round like a
crazed bullock before I gave out; and as I didn't mean to
go back . . . No. Do you see me being hauled back,
stark naked, off one of these little islands by the scruff
of the neck and fighting like a wild beast? Somebody
would have got killed for certain, and I did not want
any of that. So I went on. Then your ladder——"

"Why didn't you hail the ship?" I asked, a little
louder.

He touched my shoulder lightly. Lazy footsteps
came right over our heads and stopped. The second
mate had crossed from the other side of the poop and
might have been hanging over the rail, for all we knew.

"He couldn't hear us talking—could he?" My
double breathed into my very ear, anxiously.

His anxiety was an answer, a sufficient answer, to
the question I had put to him. An answer containing
all the difficulty of that situation. I closed the port-

hole quietly, to make sure. A louder word might have been overheard.

"Who's that?" he whispered then.

"My second mate. But I don't know much more of the fellow than you do."

And I told him a little about myself. I had been appointed to take charge while I least expected anything of the sort, not quite a fortnight ago. I didn't know either the ship or the people. Hadn't had the time in port to look about me or size anybody up. And as to the crew, all they knew was that I was appointed to take the ship home. For the rest, I was almost as much of a stranger on board as himself, I said. And at the moment I felt it most acutely. I felt that it would take very little to make me a suspect person in the eyes of the ship's company.

He had turned about meantime; and we, the two strangers in the ship, faced each other in identical attitudes.

"Your ladder——" he murmured, after a silence. "Who'd have thought of finding a ladder hanging over at night in a ship anchored out here! I felt just then a very unpleasant faintness. After the life I've been leading for nine weeks, anybody would have got out of condition. I wasn't capable of swimming round as far as your rudder-chains. And, lo and behold! there was a ladder to get hold of. After I gripped it I said to myself, 'What's the good?' When I saw a man's head looking over I thought I would swim away presently and leave him shouting—in whatever language it was. I didn't mind being looked at. I—I liked it. And then you speaking to me so quietly—as if you had expected me—made me hold on a little longer. It had been a confounded lonely time—I don't mean while swimming. I was glad to talk a little to somebody that didn't belong to the *Sephora*. As to asking for the captain, that was a mere impulse. It could have been no use, with all the ship knowing about me and the other people pretty certain to be round here in the morning. I don't know—I wanted to be seen, to talk with somebody, before I went on. I don't know what I would have said. . . . 'Fine night, isn't it?' or something of the sort."

"Do you think they will be round here presently?" I asked with some incredulity.

"Quite likely," he said, faintly.

He looked extremely haggard all of a sudden. His head rolled on his shoulders.

"H'm. We shall see then. Meantime get into that bed," I whispered. "Want help? There."

It was a rather high bed-place with a set of drawers underneath. This amazing swimmer really needed the lift I gave him by seizing his leg. He tumbled in, rolled over on his back, and flung one arm across his eyes. And then, with his face nearly hidden, he must have looked exactly as I used to look in that bed. I gazed upon my other self for a while before drawing across carefully the two green serge curtains which ran on a brass rod. I thought for a moment of pinning them together for greater safety, but I sat down on the couch, and once there I felt unwilling to rise and hunt for a pin. I would do it in a moment. I was extremely tired, in a peculiarly intimate way, by the strain of stealthiness, by the effort of whispering and the general secrecy of this excitement. It was three o'clock by now and I had been on my feet since nine, but I was not sleepy; I could not have gone to sleep. I sat there, fagged out, looking at the curtains, trying to clear my mind of the confused sensation of being in two places at once, and greatly bothered by an

exasperating knocking in my head. It was a relief to
discover suddenly that it was not in my head at all,
but on the outside of the door. Before I could collect
myself the words "Come in" were out of my mouth,
and the steward entered with a tray, bringing in my
morning coffee. I had slept, after all, and I was so
frightened that I shouted, "This way! I am here,
steward," as though he had been miles away. He put
down the tray on the table next the couch and only
then said, very quietly, "I can see you are here, sir."
I felt him give me a keen look, but I dared not meet
his eyes just then. He must have wondered why I had
drawn the curtains of my bed before going to sleep on the
couch. He went out, hooking the door open as usual.

I heard the crew washing decks above me. I knew
I would have been told at once if there had been any
wind. Calm, I thought, and I was doubly vexed.
Indeed, I felt dual more than ever. The steward
reappeared suddenly in the doorway. I jumped up
from the couch so quickly that he gave a start.

"What do you want here?"

"Close your port, sir—they are washing decks."

"It is closed," I said, reddening.

"Very well, sir." But he did not move from the
doorway and returned my stare in an extraordinary,
equivocal manner for a time. Then his eyes wavered,
all his expression changed, and in a voice unusually
gentle, almost coaxingly:

"May I come in to take the empty cup away, sir?"

"Of course!" I turned my back on him while he
popped in and out. Then I unhooked and closed the
door and even pushed the bolt. This sort of thing could
not go on very long. The cabin was as hot as an oven,
too. I took a peep at my double, and discovered that he
had not moved, his arm was still over his eyes; but his

chest heaved; his hair was wet; his chin glistened with perspiration. I reached over him and opened the port.

"I must show myself on deck," I reflected.

Of course, theoretically, I could do what I liked, with no one to say nay to me within the whole circle of the horizon; but to lock my cabin door and take the key away I did not dare. Directly I put my head out of the companion I saw the group of my two officers, the second mate barefooted, the chief mate in long india-rubber boots, near the break of the poop, and the steward half-way down the poop-ladder talking to them eagerly. He happened to catch sight of me and dived, the second ran down on the main-deck shouting some order or other, and the chief mate came to meet me, touching his cap.

There was a sort of curiosity in his eye that I did not like. I don't know whether the steward had told them that I was "queer" only, or downright drunk, but I know the man meant to have a good look at me. I watched him coming with a smile which, as he got into point-blank range, took effect and froze his very whiskers. I did not give him time to open his lips.

"Square the yards by lifts and braces before the hands go to breakfast."

It was the first particular order I had given on board that ship; and I stayed on deck to see it executed, too. I had felt the need of asserting myself without loss of time. That sneering young cub got taken down a peg or two on that occasion, and I also seized the opportunity of having a good look at the face of every foremast man as they filed past me to go to the after braces. At breakfast time, eating nothing myself, I presided with such frigid dignity that the two mates were only too glad to escape from the cabin as soon as decency permitted; and all the time the dual working of my mind distracted me almost to the point of insanity. I was constantly watching myself, my secret self, as dependent on my actions as my own personality, sleeping in that bed, behind that door which faced me as I sat at the head of the table. It was very much like being mad, only it was worse because one was aware of it.

I had to shake him for a solid minute, but when at last he opened his eyes it was in the full possession of his senses, with an inquiring look.

"All's well so far," I whispered. "Now you must vanish into the bath-room."

He did so, as noiseless as a ghost, and then I rang for the steward, and facing him boldly, directed him to tidy up my stateroom while I was having my bath—"and be quick about it." As my tone admitted of no excuses, he said, "Yes, sir," and ran off to fetch his dust-pan and brushes. I took a bath and did most of my dressing, splashing, and whistling softly for the steward's edification, while the secret sharer of my life stood drawn up bolt upright in that little space, his face looking very sunken in daylight, his eyelids lowered under the stern, dark line of his eyebrows drawn together by a slight frown.

When I left him there to go back to my room the steward was finishing dusting. I sent for the mate and engaged him in some insignificant conversation. It was, as it were, trifling with the terrific character of his whiskers; but my object was to give him an opportunity for a good look at my cabin. And then I could at last shut, with a clear conscience, the door of my stateroom and get my double back into the recessed part. There was nothing else for it. He had to sit still on a small folding stool, half smothered by the heavy coats hanging there. We listened to the

teward going into the bath-room out of the saloon,
illing the water-bottles there, scrubbing the bath,
etting things to rights, whisk, bang, clatter—out again
nto the saloon—turn the key—click. Such was my
cheme for keeping my second self invisible. Nothing
etter could be contrived under the circumstances.
And there we sat; I at my writing-desk ready to appear
usy with some papers, he behind me out of sight of the
oor. It would not have been prudent to talk in day-
ime; and I could not have stood the excitement of that
queer sense of whispering to myself. Now and then,
lancing over my shoulder, I saw him far back there,
itting rigidly on the low stool, his bare feet close to-
ether, his arms folded, his head hanging on his breast—
ind perfectly still. Anybody would have taken him for
ne.

I was fascinated by it myself. Every moment I
ad to glance over my shoulder. I was looking at him
vhen a voice outside the door said:

"Beg pardon, sir."

"Well!" . . . I kept my eyes on him, and so
vhen the voice outside the door announced, "There's
, ship's boat coming our way, sir," I saw him give a
tart—the first movement he had made for hours. But
e did not raise his bowed head.

"All right. Get the ladder over."

I hesitated. Should I whisper something to him?
But what? His immobility seemed to have been never
isturbed. What could I tell him he did not know
lready? . . . Finally I went on deck.

II

THE skipper of the *Sephora* had a thin red whisker all
ound his face, and the sort of complexion that goes

with hair of that colour; also the particular, rather smeary shade of blue in the eyes. He was not exactly a showy figure; his shoulders were high, his stature but middling—one leg slightly more bandy than the other. He shook hands, looking vaguely around. A spiritless tenacity was his main characteristic, I judged. I behaved with a politeness which seemed to disconcert him. Perhaps he was shy. He mumbled to me as if he were ashamed of what he was saying; gave his name (it was something like Archbold—but at this distance of years I hardly am sure), his ship's name, and a few other particulars of that sort, in the manner of a criminal making a reluctant and doleful confession. He had had terrible weather on the passage out—terrible— terrible—wife aboard, too.

By this time we were seated in the cabin and the steward brought in a tray with a bottle and glasses. "Thanks! No." Never took liquor. Would have some water, though. He drank two tumblerfuls. Terrible thirsty work. Ever since daylight had been exploring the islands round his ship.

"What was that for—fun?" I asked, with an appearance of polite interest.

"No!" He sighed. "Painful duty."

As he persisted in his mumbling and I wanted my double to hear every word, I hit upon the notion of informing him that I regretted to say I was hard of hearing.

"Such a young man, too!" he nodded, keeping his smeary blue, unintelligent eyes fastened upon me. "What was the cause of it—some disease?" he inquired, without the least sympathy and as if he thought that, if so, I'd got no more than I deserved.

"Yes; disease," I admitted in a cheerful tone which seemed to shock him. But my point was gained, because he had to raise his voice to give me his tale. It is not worth while to record that version. It was just over two months since all this had happened, and he had thought so much about it that he seemed completely muddled as to its bearings, but still immensely impressed.

"What would you think of such a thing happening on board your own ship? I've had the *Sephora* for these fifteen years. I am a well-known shipmaster."

He was densely distressed—and perhaps I should have sympathised with him if I had been able to detach my mental vision from the unsuspected sharer of my cabin as though he were my second self. There he was on the other side of the bulkhead, four or five feet from us, no more, as we sat in the saloon. I looked politely at Captain Archbold (if that was his name), but it was the other I saw, in a grey sleeping-suit, seated on a low stool, his bare feet close together, his arms folded, and every word said between us falling into the ears of his dark head bowed on his chest.

"I have been at sea now, man and boy, for seven-and-thirty years, and I've never heard of such a thing happening in an English ship. And that it should be my ship. Wife on board, too."

I was hardly listening to him.

"Don't you think," I said, "that the heavy sea which, you told me, came aboard just then might have killed the man? I have seen the sheer weight of a sea kill a man very neatly, by simply breaking his neck."

"Good God!" he uttered, impressively, fixing his smeary blue eyes on me. "The sea! No man killed by the sea ever looked like that." He seemed positively scandalised at my suggestion. And as I gazed at him, certainly not prepared for anything original on his part, he advanced his head close to mine and thrust his tongue out at me so suddenly that I couldn't help starting back.

After scoring over my calmness in this graphic way he nodded wisely. If I had seen the sight, he assured me, I would never forget it as long as I lived. The weather was too bad to give the corpse a proper sea burial. So next day at dawn they took it up on the poop, covering its face with a bit of bunting; he read a short prayer, and then, just as it was, in its oilskins and long boots, they launched it amongst those mountainous seas that seemed ready every moment to swallow up the ship herself and the terrified lives on board of her.

"That reefed foresail saved you," I threw in.

"Under God—it did," he exclaimed fervently. "It was by a special mercy, I firmly believe, that it stood some of those hurricane squalls."

"It was the setting of that sail which——" I began.

"God's own hand in it," he interrupted me. "Nothing less could have done it. I don't mind telling you that I hardly dared give the order. It seemed impossible that we could touch anything without losing it, and then our last hope would have been gone."

The terror of that gale was on him yet. I let him go on for a bit, then said, casually—as if returning to a minor subject:

"You were very anxious to give up your mate to the shore people, I believe?"

He was. To the law. His obscure tenacity on that point had in it something incomprehensible and a little awful; something, as it were, mystical, quite apart from his anxiety that he should not be suspected of "countenancing any doings of that sort." Seven-and-thirty virtuous years at sea, of which over twenty of immaculate command, and the last fifteen in the *Sephora*,

seemed to have laid him under some pitiless obliga-
tion.

"And you know," he went on, groping shamefacedly
amongst his feelings, "I did not engage that young
fellow. His people had some interest with my owners.
I was in a way forced to take him on. He looked very
smart, very gentlemanly, and all that. But do you
know—I never liked him, somehow. I am a plain
man. You see, he wasn't exactly the sort for the
chief mate of a ship like the *Sephora*."

I had become so connected in thoughts and impressions with the secret sharer of my cabin that I
felt as if I, personally, were being given to understand
that I, too, was not the sort that would have done
for the chief mate of a ship like the *Sephora*. I had no
doubt of it in my mind.

"Not at all the style of man. You understand,"
he insisted, superfluously, looking hard at me.

I smiled urbanely. He seemed at a loss for a while.

"I suppose I must report a suicide."

"Beg pardon?"

"Sui-cide! That's what I'll have to write to my
owners directly I get in."

"Unless you manage to recover him before to-morrow,"
I assented, dispassionately. . . . "I mean, alive."

He mumbled something which I really did not catch,
and I turned my ear to him in a puzzled manner. He
fairly bawled:

"The land—I say, the mainland is at least seven
miles off my anchorage."

"About that."

My lack of excitement, of curiosity, of surprise, of
any sort of pronounced interest, began to arouse his
distrust. But except for the felicitous pretence of
deafness I had not tried to pretend anything. I had

felt utterly incapable of playing the part of ignorance properly, and therefore was afraid to try. It is also certain that he had brought some ready-made suspicions with him, and that he viewed my politeness as a strange and unnatural phenomenon. And yet how else could I have received him? Not heartily! That was impossible for psychological reasons, which I need not state here. My only object was to keep off his inquiries. Surlily? Yes, but surliness might have provoked a point-blank question. From its novelty to him and from its nature, punctilious courtesy was the manner best calculated to restrain the man. But there was the danger of his breaking through my defence bluntly. I could not, I think, have met him by a direct lie, also for psychological (not moral) reasons. If he had only known how afraid I was of his putting my feeling of identity with the other to the test! But, strangely enough—(I thought of it only afterwards)—I believe that he was not a little disconcerted by the reverse side of that weird situation, by something in me that reminded him of the man he was seeking—suggested a mysterious similitude to the young fellow he had distrusted and disliked from the first.

However that might have been, the silence was not very prolonged. He took another oblique step.

"I reckon I had no more than a two-mile pull to your ship. Not a bit more."

"And quite enough, too, in this awful heat," I said.

Another pause full of mistrust followed. Necessity, they say, is mother of invention, but fear, too, is not barren of ingenious suggestions. And I was afraid he would ask me point-blank for news of my other self.

"Nice little saloon, isn't it?" I remarked, as if noticing for the first time the way his eyes roamed from one closed door to the other. "And very well fitted out, too. Here, for instance," I continued, reaching over the back of my seat negligently and flinging the door open, "is my bath-room."

He made an eager movement, but hardly gave it a glance. I got up, shut the door of the bath-room, and invited him to have a look round, as if I were very proud of my accommodation. He had to rise and be shown round, but he went through the business without any raptures whatever.

"And now we'll have a look at my stateroom," I declared, in a voice as loud as I dared to make it, crossing the cabin to the starboard side with purposely heavy steps.

He followed me in and gazed around. My intelligent double had vanished. I played my part.

"Very convenient—isn't it?"

"Very nice. Very comf . . ." He didn't finish and went out brusquely as if to escape from some unrighteous wiles of mine. But it was not to be. I had been too frightened not to feel vengeful; I felt I had him on the run, and I meant to keep him on the run. My polite insistence must have had something menacing in it, because he gave in suddenly. And I did not let him off a single item; mate's room, pantry, storerooms, the very sail-locker which was also under the poop—he had to look into them all. When at last I showed him out on the quarter-deck he drew a long, spiritless sigh, and mumbled dismally that he must really be going back to his ship now. I desired my mate, who had joined us, to see to the captain's boat.

The man of whiskers gave a blast on the whistle which he used to wear hanging round his neck, and yelled, "*Sephora's* away!" My double down there in my cabin must have heard, and certainly could not feel more relieved than I. Four fellows came running out from somewhere forward and went over the side, while my own men, appearing on deck too, lined the rail. I escorted my visitor to the gangway ceremoniously, and nearly overdid it. He was a tenacious beast. On the very ladder he lingered, and in that unique, guiltily conscientious manner of sticking to the point:

"I say . . . you . . . you don't think that——"

I covered his voice loudly:

"Certainly not. . . . I am delighted. Good-bye."

I had an idea of what he meant to say, and just saved myself by the privilege of defective hearing. He was too shaken generally to insist, but my mate, close witness of that parting, looked mystified and his face took on a thoughtful cast. As I did not want to appear as if I wished to avoid all communication with my officers, he had the opportunity to address me.

"Seems a very nice man. His boat's crew told our chaps a very extraordinary story, if what I am told by the steward is true. I suppose you had it from the captain, sir?"

"Yes. I had a story from the captain."

"A very horrible affair—isn't it, sir?"

"It is."

"Beats all these tales we hear about murders in Yankee ships."

"I don't think it beats them. I don't think it resembles them in the least."

"Bless my soul—you don't say so! But of course I've no acquaintance whatever with American ships, not I, so I couldn't go against your knowledge. It's horrible enough for me. . . . But the queerest part is that those fellows seemed to have some idea the man was hidden aboard here. They had really. Did you ever hear of such a thing?"

"Preposterous—isn't it?"

We were walking to and fro athwart the quarter-deck. No one of the crew forward could be seen (the day was Sunday), and the mate pursued:

"There was some little dispute about it. Our chaps took offence. 'As if we would harbour a thing like that,' they said. 'Wouldn't you like to look for him in our coal-hole?' Quite a tiff. But they made it up in the end. I suppose he did drown himself. Don't you, sir?"

"I don't suppose anything."

"You have no doubt in the matter, sir?"

"None whatever."

I left him suddenly. I felt I was producing a bad impression, but with my double down there it was most trying to be on deck. And it was almost as trying to be below. Altogether a nerve-trying situation. But on the whole I felt less torn in two when I was with him. There was no one in the whole ship whom I dared take into my confidence. Since the hands had got to know his story, it would have been impossible to pass him off for any one else, and an accidental discovery was to be dreaded now more than ever. . . .

The steward being engaged in laying the table for dinner, we could talk only with our eyes when I first went down. Later in the afternoon we had a cautious try at whispering. The Sunday quietness of the ship was against us; the stillness of air and water around her was against us; the elements, the men were against us—everything was against us in our secret partnership; time itself—for this could not go on forever. The very trust in Providence was, I suppose, denied to his guilt. Shall I confess that this thought cast me down very much? And as to the chapter of accidents which counts for so much in the book of success, I could only hope that it was closed. For what favourable accident could be expected?

"Did you hear everything?" were my first words as soon as we took up our position side by side, leaning over my bed-place.

He had. And the proof of it was his earnest whisper, "The man told you he hardly dared to give the order."

I understood the reference to be to that saving fore-sail.

"Yes. He was afraid of it being lost in the setting."

"I assure you he never gave the order. He may think he did, but he never gave it. He stood there with me on the break of the poop after the maintopsail blew away, and whimpered about our last hope—positively whimpered about it and nothing else—and the night coming on! To hear one's skipper go on like that in such weather was enough to drive any fellow out of his mind. It worked me up into a sort of desper-ation. I just took it into my own hands and went away from him, boiling, and—— But what's the use telling you? *You* know! . . . Do you think that if I had not been pretty fierce with them I should have got the men to do anything? Not it! The bo's'n perhaps? Perhaps! It wasn't a heavy sea—it was a sea gone mad! I suppose the end of the world will be some-thing like that; and a man may have the heart to see it coming once and be done with it—but to have to face it day after day—— I don't blame anybody. I was precious little better than the rest. Only—I was an officer of that old coal-wagon, anyhow——"

"I quite understand," I conveyed that sincere assurance into his ear. He was out of breath with whispering; I could hear him pant slightly. It was all very simple. The same strung-up force which had given twenty-four men a chance, at least, for their lives, had, in a sort of recoil, crushed an unworthy mutinous existence.

But I had no leisure to weigh the merits of the matter—footsteps in the saloon, a heavy knock. "There's enough wind to get under way with, sir." Here was the call of a new claim upon my thoughts and even upon my feelings.

"Turn the hands up," I cried through the door. "I'll be on deck directly."

I was going out to make the acquaintance of my ship. Before I left the cabin our eyes met—the eyes of the only two strangers on board. I pointed to the recessed part where the little camp-stool awaited him and laid my finger on my lips. He made a gesture—somewhat vague—a little mysterious, accompanied by a faint smile, as if of regret.

This is not the place to enlarge upon the sensations of a man who feels for the first time a ship move under his feet to his own independent word. In my case they were not unalloyed. I was not wholly alone with my command; for there was that stranger in my cabin. Or rather, I was not completely and wholly with her. Part of me was absent. That mental feeling of being in two places at once affected me physically as if the mood of secrecy had penetrated my very soul. Before an hour had elapsed since the ship had begun to move, having occasion to ask the mate (he stood by my side) to take a compass bearing of the Pagoda, I caught myself reaching up to his ear in whispers. I say I caught myself, but enough had escaped to startle the man. I can't describe it otherwise than by saying that he shied. A grave, preoccupied manner, as though he were in possession of some perplexing intelligence, did not leave him henceforth. A little later I moved away from the rail to look at the compass with such a stealthy gait that the helmsman noticed it —and I could not help noticing the unusual roundness of his eyes. These are trifling instances, though it's to no commander's advantage to be suspected of ludicrous eccentricities. But I was also more seriously affected. There are to a seaman certain words, gestures, that should in given conditions come as naturally, as instinctively as the winking of a menaced eye. A certain order should spring on to his lips without thinking; a certain sign should get itself made, so to speak, without reflection. But all unconscious alertness had abandoned me. I had to make an effort of will to recall myself back (from the cabin) to the conditions of the moment. I felt that I was appearing an irresolute commander to those people who were watching me more or less critically.

And, besides, there were the scares. On the second day out, for instance, coming off the deck in the afternoon (I had straw slippers on my bare feet) I stopped at the open pantry door and spoke to the steward. He was doing something there with his back to me. At the sound of my voice he nearly jumped out of his skin, as the saying is, and incidentally broke a cup.

"What on earth's the matter with you?" I asked, astonished.

He was extremely confused. "Beg your pardon, sir. I made sure you were in your cabin."

"You see I wasn't."

"No, sir. I could have sworn I had heard you moving in there not a moment ago. It's most extraordinary . . . very sorry, sir."

I passed on with an inward shudder. I was so identified with my secret double that I did not even mention the fact in those scanty, fearful whispers we exchanged. I suppose he had made some slight noise

of some kind or other. It would have been miraculous
if he hadn't at one time or another. And yet, haggard
as he appeared, he looked always perfectly self-
controlled, more than calm—almost invulnerable. On
my suggestion he remained almost entirely in the bath-
room, which, upon the whole, was the safest place.
There could be really no shadow of an excuse for any one
ever wanting to go in there, once the steward had
done with it. It was a very tiny place. Sometimes
he reclined on the floor, his legs bent, his head sustained
on one elbow. At others I would find him on the camp-
stool, sitting in his grey sleeping-suit and with his
cropped dark hair like a patient, unmoved convict. At
night I would smuggle him into my bed-place, and we
would whisper together, with the regular footfalls of the
officer of the watch passing and repassing over our
heads. It was an infinitely miserable time. It was
lucky that some tins of fine preserves were stowed in
a locker in my stateroom; hard bread I could always
get hold of; and so he lived on stewed chicken, paté de
foie gras, asparagus, cooked oysters, sardines—on all
sorts of abominable sham delicacies out of tins. My
early morning coffee he always drank; and it was all I
dared do for him in that respect.

Every day there was the horrible manœuvring to go
through so that my room and then the bath-room
should be done in the usual way. I came to hate the
sight of the steward, to abhor the voice of that harmless
man. I felt that it was he who would bring on the
disaster of discovery. It hung like a sword over our
heads.

The fourth day out, I think (we were then working
down the east side of the Gulf of Siam, tack for tack,
in light winds and smooth water)—the fourth day, I
say, of this miserable juggling with the unavoidable, as

we sat at our evening meal, that man, whose slightest movement I dreaded, after putting down the dishes ran up on deck busily. This could not be dangerous. Presently he came down again; and then it appeared that he had remembered a coat of mine which I had thrown over a rail to dry after having been wetted in a shower which had passed over the ship in the afternoon. Sitting stolidly at the head of the table I became terrified at the sight of the garment on his arm. Of course he made for my door. There was no time to lose.

"Steward," I thundered. My nerves were so shaken that I could not govern my voice and conceal my agitation. This was the sort of thing that made my terrifically whiskered mate tap his forehead with his forefinger. I had detected him using that gesture while talking on deck with a confidential air to the carpenter. It was too far to hear a word, but I had no doubt that this pantomime could only refer to the strange new captain.

"Yes, sir," the pale-faced steward turned resignedly to me. It was this maddening course of being shouted at, checked without rhyme or reason, arbitrarily chased out of my cabin, suddenly called into it, sent flying out of his pantry on incomprehensible errands, that accounted for the growing wretchedness of his expression.

"Where are you going with that coat?"

"To your room, sir."

"Is there another shower coming?"

"I'm sure I don't know, sir. Shall I go up again and see, sir?"

"No! never mind."

My object was attained, as of course my other self in there would have heard everything that passed.

During this interlude my two officers never raised their eyes off their respective plates; but the lip of that confounded cub, the second mate, quivered visibly.

I expected the steward to hook my coat on and come out at once. He was very slow about it; but I dominated my nervousness sufficiently not to shout after him. Suddenly I became aware (it could be heard plainly enough) that the fellow for some reason or other was opening the door of the bath-room. It was the end. The place was literally not big enough to swing a cat in. My voice died in my throat and I went stony all over. I expected to hear a yell of surprise and terror, and made a movement, but had not the strength to get on my legs. Everything remained still. Had my second self taken the poor wretch by the throat? I don't know what I could have done next moment if I had not seen the steward come out of my room, close the door, and then stand quietly by the sideboard.

"Saved," I thought. "But, no! Lost! Gone! He was gone!"

I laid my knife and fork down and leaned back in my chair. My head swam. After a while, when sufficiently recovered to speak in a steady voice, I instructed my mate to put the ship round at eight o'clock himself.

"I won't come on deck," I went on. "I think I'll turn in, and unless the wind shifts I don't want to be disturbed before midnight. I feel a bit seedy."

"You did look middling bad a little while ago," the chief mate remarked without showing any great concern.

They both went out, and I stared at the steward clearing the table. There was nothing to be read on that wretched man's face. But why did he avoid my eyes I asked myself. Then I thought I should like to hear the sound of his voice.

"Steward!"

"Sir!" Startled as usual.

"Where did you hang up that coat?"

"In the bath-room, sir." The usual anxious tone. "It's not quite dry yet, sir."

For some time longer I sat in the cuddy. Had my double vanished as he had come? But of his coming there was an explanation, whereas his disappearance would be inexplicable. . . . I went slowly into my dark room, shut the door, lighted the lamp, and for a time dared not turn round. When at last I did I saw him standing bolt-upright in the narrow recessed part. It would not be true to say I had a shock, but an irresistible doubt of his bodily existence flitted through my mind. Can it be, I asked myself, that he is not visible to other eyes than mine? It was like being haunted. Motionless, with a grave face, he raised his hands slightly at me in a gesture which meant clearly, "Heavens! what a narrow escape!" Narrow indeed. I think I had come creeping quietly as near insanity as any man who has not actually gone over the border. That gesture restrained me, so to speak.

The mate with the terrific whiskers was now putting the ship on the other tack. In the moment of profound silence which follows upon the hands going to their stations I heard on the poop his raised voice: "Hard alee!" and the distant shout of the order repeated on the maindeck. The sails, in that light breeze, made but a faint fluttering noise. It ceased. The ship was coming round slowly; I held my breath in the renewed stillness of expectation; one wouldn't have thought that there was a single living soul on her decks. A sudden brisk shout, "Mainsail haul!" broke the spell, and in the noisy cries and rush overhead of the men running away with the main-brace we two, down in my cabin, came together in our usual position by the bed-place.

He did not wait for my question. "I heard him fumbling here and just managed to squat myself down in the bath," he whispered to me. "The fellow only opened the door and put his arm in to hang the coat up. All the same——"

"I never thought of that," I whispered back, even more appalled than before at the closeness of the shave, and marvelling at that something unyielding in his character which was carrying him through so finely. There was no agitation in his whisper. Whoever was being driven distracted, it was not he. He was sane. And the proof of his sanity was continued when he took up the whispering again.

"It would never do for me to come to life again."

It was something that a ghost might have said. But what he was alluding to was his old captain's reluctant admission of the theory of suicide. It would obviously serve his turn—if I had understood at all the view which seemed to govern the unalterable purpose of his action.

"You must maroon me as soon as ever you can get amongst these islands off the Cambodge shore," he went on.

"Maroon you! We are not living in a boy's adventure tale," I protested. His scornful whispering took me up.

"We aren't indeed! There's nothing of a boy's tale in this. But there's nothing else for it. I want no more. You don't suppose I am afraid of what can be done to me? Prison or gallows or whatever they may please. But you don't see me coming back to explain such things to an old fellow in a wig and twelve respectable tradesmen, do you? What can they know whether I am guilty or not—or of *what* I am guilty, either? That's my affair. What does the Bible say? 'Driven off the face of the earth.' Very well. I am off the face of the earth now. As I came at night so I shall go."

"Impossible!" I murmured. "You can't."

"Can't? . . . Not naked like a soul on the Day of Judgment. I shall freeze on to this sleeping-suit. The Last Day is not yet—and . . . you have understood thoroughly. Didn't you?"

I felt suddenly ashamed of myself. I may say truly that I understood—and my hesitation in letting that man swim away from my ship's side had been a mere sham sentiment, a sort of cowardice.

"It can't be done now till next night," I breathed out. "The ship is on the off-shore tack and the wind may fail us."

"As long as I know that you understand," he whispered. "But of course you do. It's a great satisfaction to have got somebody to understand. You seem to have been there on purpose." And in the same whisper, as if we two whenever we talked had to say things to each other which were not fit for the world to hear, he added, "It's very wonderful."

We remained side by side talking in our secret way —but sometimes silent or just exchanging a whispered word or two at long intervals. And as usual he stared through the port. A breath of wind came now and again into our faces. The ship might have been moored in dock, so gently and on an even keel she slipped through the water, that did not murmur even at our passage, shadowy and silent like a phantom sea.

At midnight I went on deck, and to my mate's great surprise put the ship round on the other tack. His terrible whiskers flitted round me in silent criticism. I certainly should not have done it if it had been only a question of getting out of that sleepy gulf as quickly as possible. I believe he told the second mate, who relieved him, that it was a great want of judgment. The other only yawned. That intolerable cub shuffled about so sleepily and lolled against the rails in such a slack, improper fashion that I came down on him sharply.

"Aren't you properly awake yet?"

"Yes, sir! I am awake."

"Well, then, be good enough to hold yourself as if you were. And keep a look-out. If there's any current we'll be closing with some islands before daylight."

The east side of the gulf is fringed with islands, some solitary, others in groups. On the blue background of the high coast they seem to float on silvery patches of calm water, arid and grey, or dark green and rounded like clumps of evergreen bushes, with the larger ones, a mile or two long, showing the outlines of ridges, ribs of grey rock under the dank mantle of matted leafage. Unknown to trade, to travel, almost to geography, the manner of life they harbour is an unsolved secret. There must be villages—settlements of fishermen at least—on the largest of them, and some communication with the world is probably kept up by native craft. But all that forenoon, as we headed for them, fanned along by the faintest of breezes, I saw no sign of man or canoe in the field of the telescope I kept on pointing at the scattered group.

At noon I gave no orders for a change of course, and the mate's whiskers became much concerned and seemed to be offering themselves unduly to my notice. At last I said:

"I am going to stand right in. Quite in—as far as I can take her."

The stare of extreme surprise imparted an air of ferocity also to his eyes, and he looked truly terrific for a moment.

"We're not doing well in the middle of the gulf," I continued, casually. "I am going to look for the land breezes to-night."

"Bless my soul! Do you mean, sir, in the dark amongst the lot of all them islands and reefs and shoals?"

"Well—if there are any regular land breezes at all on this coast one must get close inshore to find them, mustn't one?"

"Bless my soul!" he exclaimed again under his breath. All that afternoon he wore a dreamy, contemplative appearance which in him was a mark of perplexity. After dinner I went into my stateroom as if I meant to take some rest. There we two bent our dark heads over a half-unrolled chart lying on my bed.

"There," I said. "It's got to be Koh-ring. I've been looking at it ever since sunrise. It has got two hills and a low point. It must be inhabited. And on the coast opposite there is what looks like the mouth of a biggish river—with some town, no doubt, not far up. It's the best chance for you that I can see."

"Anything. Koh-ring let it be."

He looked thoughtfully at the chart as if surveying chances and distances from a lofty height—and following with his eyes his own figure wandering on the blank land of Cochin-China, and then passing off that piece of paper clean out of sight into uncharted regions. And it was as if the ship had two captains to plan her course for her. I had been so worried and restless running up and down that I had not had the patience to dress that day. I had remained in my sleeping-suit, with straw slippers and a soft floppy hat. The closeness of the heat in the gulf had been most oppressive, and the crew were used to see me wandering in that airy attire.

"She will clear the south point as she heads now," I whispered into his ear. "Goodness only knows when, though, but certainly after dark. I'll edge her in to half a mile, as far as I may be able to judge in the dark——"

"Be careful," he murmured, warningly—and I realised suddenly that all my future, the only future for which I was fit, would perhaps go irretrievably to pieces in any mishap to my first command.

I could not stop a moment longer in the room. I motioned him to get out of sight and made my way on the poop. That unplayful cub had the watch. I walked up and down for a while thinking things out, then beckoned him over.

"Send a couple of hands to open the two quarter-deck ports," I said, mildly.

He actually had the impudence, or else so forgot himself in his wonder at such an incomprehensible order, as to repeat:

"Open the quarter-deck ports! What for, sir?"

"The only reason you need concern yourself about is because I tell you to do so. Have them opened wide and fastened properly."

He reddened and went off, but I believe made some jeering remark to the carpenter as to the sensible practice of ventilating a ship's quarter-deck. I know he popped into the mate's cabin to impart the fact to him because the whiskers came on deck, as it were by chance, and stole glances at me from below—for signs of lunacy or drunkenness, I suppose.

A little before supper, feeling more restless than ever, I rejoined, for a moment, my second self. And to find him sitting so quietly was surprising, like something against nature, inhuman.

I developed my plan in a hurried whisper.

"I shall stand in as close as I dare and then put her round. I will presently find means to smuggle you out of here into the sail-locker, which communicates with the lobby. But there is an opening, a sort of square for hauling the sails out, which gives straight on the quarter-deck and which is never closed in fine weather, so as to give air to the sails. When the ship's way is deadened in stays and all the hands are aft at the main-braces you will have a clear road to slip out and get overboard through the open quarter-deck port. I've had them both fastened up. Use a rope's end to lower yourself into the water so as to avoid a splash— you know. It could be heard and cause some beastly complication."

He kept silent for a while, then whispered, "I understand."

"I won't be there to see you go," I began with an effort. "The rest . . . I only hope I have understood, too."

"You have. From first to last"—and for the first time there seemed to be a faltering, something strained in his whisper. He caught hold of my arm, but the ringing of the supper bell made me start. He didn't, though; he only released his grip.

After supper I didn't come below again till well past eight o'clock. The faint, steady breeze was loaded with dew; and the wet, darkened sails held all there was of propelling power in it. The night, clear and starry, sparkled darkly, and the opaque, lightless patches shifting slowly against the low stars were the drifting islets. On the port bow there was a big one more distant and shadowily imposing by the great space of sky it eclipsed.

On opening the door I had a back view of my very own self looking at a chart. He had come out of the recess and was standing near the table.

"Quite dark enough," I whispered.

He stepped back and leaned against my bed with a level, quiet glance. I sat on the couch. We had nothing to say to each other. Over our heads the officer of the watch moved here and there. Then I heard him move quickly. I knew what that meant. He was making for the companion; and presently his voice was outside my door.

"We are drawing in pretty fast, sir. Land looks rather close."

"Very well," I answered. "I am coming on deck directly."

I waited till he was gone out of the cuddy, then rose. My double moved too. The time had come to exchange our last whispers, for neither of us was ever to hear each other's natural voice.

"Look here!" I opened a drawer and took out three sovereigns. "Take this anyhow. I've got six and I'd give you the lot, only I must keep a little money to buy some fruit and vegetables for the crew from native boats as we go through Sunda Straits."

He shook his head.

"Take it," I urged him, whispering desperately. "No one can tell what——"

He smiled and slapped meaningly the only pocket of the sleeping-jacket. It was not safe, certainly. But I produced a large old silk handkerchief of mine, and tying the three pieces of gold in a corner, pressed it on him. He was touched, I suppose, because he took it at last and tied it quickly round his waist under the jacket, on his bare skin.

Our eyes met; several seconds elapsed, till, our glances still mingled, I extended my hand and turned the lamp out. Then I passed through the cuddy, leaving the door of my room wide open. . . . "Steward!"

He was still lingering in the pantry in the greatness of his zeal, giving a rub-up to a plated cruet stand the last thing before going to bed. Being careful not to wake up the mate, whose room was opposite, I spoke in an undertone.

He looked round anxiously. "Sir!"

"Can you get me a little hot water from the galley?"

"I am afraid, sir, the galley fire's been out for some time now."

"Go and see."

He flew up the stairs.

"Now," I whispered, loudly, into the saloon—too loudly, perhaps, but I was afraid I couldn't make a sound. He was by my side in an instant—the double captain slipped past the stairs—through a tiny dark passage . . . a sliding door. We were in the sail-locker, scrambling on our knees over the sails. A sudden thought struck me. I saw myself wandering barefooted, bareheaded, the sun beating on my dark poll. I snatched off my floppy hat and tried hurriedly in the dark to ram it on my other self. He dodged and fended off silently. I wonder what he thought had come to me before he understood and suddenly desisted. Our hands met gropingly, lingered united in a steady, motionless clasp for a second. . . . No word was breathed by either of us when they separated.

I was standing quietly by the pantry door when the steward returned.

"Sorry, sir. Kettle barely warm. Shall I light the spirit-lamp?"

"Never mind."

I came out on deck slowly. It was now a matter of conscience to shave the land as close as possible—for now he must go overboard whenever the ship was put in stays. Must! There could be no going back for him. After a moment I walked over to leeward and my heart flew into my mouth at the nearness of the land on the bow. Under any other circumstances I would not have held on a minute longer. The second mate had followed me anxiously.

I looked on till I felt I could command my voice.

"She will weather," I said then in a quiet tone.

"Are you going to try that, sir?" he stammered out incredulously.

I took no notice of him and raised my tone just enough to be heard by the helmsman.

"Keep her good full."

"Good full, sir."

The wind fanned my cheek, the sails slept, the world was silent. The strain of watching the dark loom of the land grow bigger and denser was too much for me. I had shut my eyes—because the ship must go closer. She must! The stillness was intolerable. Were we standing still?

When I opened my eyes the second view started my heart with a thump. The black southern hill of Koh-ring seemed to hang right over the ship like a towering fragment of the everlasting night. On that enormous mass of blackness there was not a gleam to be seen, not a sound to be heard. It was gliding irresistibly towards us and yet seemed already within reach of the hand. I saw the vague figures of the watch grouped in the waist, gazing in awed silence.

"Are you going on, sir?" inquired an unsteady voice at my elbow.

I ignored it. I had to go on.

"Keep her full. Don't check her way. That won't do now," I said, warningly.

"I can't see the sails very well," the helmsman answered me, in strange, quavering tones.

Was she close enough? Already she was, I won't say in the shadow of the land, but in the very blackness of it, already swallowed up as it were, gone too close to be recalled, gone from me altogether.

"Give the mate a call," I said to the young man who stood at my elbow as still as death. "And turn all hands up."

My tone had a borrowed loudness reverberated from the height of the land. Several voices cried out together: "We are all on deck, sir."

Then stillness again, with the great shadow gliding closer, towering higher, without a light, without a sound. Such a hush had fallen on the ship that she might have been a bark of the dead floating in slowly under the very gate of Erebus.

"My God! Where are we?"

It was the mate moaning at my elbow. He was thunderstruck, and as it were deprived of the moral support of his whiskers. He clapped his hands and absolutely cried out, "Lost!"

"Be quiet," I said, sternly.

He lowered his tone, but I saw the shadowy gesture of his despair. "What are we doing here?"

"Looking for the land wind."

He made as if to tear his hair, and addressed me recklessly.

"She will never get out. You have done it, sir. I knew it'd end in something like this. She will never

weather, and you are too close now to stay. She'll
drift ashore before she's round. O my God!"

I caught his arm as he was raising it to batter his
poor devoted head, and shook it violently.

"She's ashore already," he wailed, trying to tear
himself away.

"Is she? . . . Keep good full there!"

"Good full, sir," cried the helmsman in a frightened,
thin, child-like voice.

I hadn't let go the mate's arm and went on shaking
it. "Ready about, do you hear? You go forward"
—shake—"and stop there"—shake—" and hold your
noise"—shake—"and see these head-sheets properly
overhauled"—shake, shake—shake.

And all the time I dared not look towards the land
lest my heart should fail me. I released my grip at last
and he ran forward as if fleeing for dear life.

I wondered what my double there in the sail-locker
thought of this commotion. He was able to hear
everything—and perhaps he was able to understand
why, on my conscience, it had to be thus close—no
less. My first order "Hard alee!" re-echoed ominously
under the towering shadow of Koh-ring as if I had
shouted in a mountain gorge. And then I watched
the land intently. In that smooth water and light
wind it was impossible to feel the ship coming-to. No!
I could not feel her. And my second self was making
now ready to slip out and lower himself overboard.
Perhaps he was gone already . . . ?

The great black mass brooding over our very mastheads began to pivot away from the ship's side silently.
And now I forgot the secret stranger ready to depart,
and remembered only that I was a total stranger to
the ship. I did not know her. Would she do it?
How was she to be handled?

I swung the mainyard and waited helplessly. She was perhaps stopped, and her very fate hung in the balance, with the black mass of Koh-ring like the gate of the everlasting night towering over her taffrail. What would she do now? Had she way on her yet? I stepped to the side swiftly, and on the shadowy water I could see nothing except a faint phosphorescent flash revealing the glassy smoothness of the sleeping surface. It was impossible to tell—and I had not learned yet the feel of my ship. Was she moving? What I needed was something easily seen, a piece of paper, which I could throw overboard and watch. I had nothing on me. To run down for it I didn't dare. There was no time. All at once my strained, yearning stare distinguished a white object floating within a yard of the ship's side. White on the black water. A phosphorescent flash passed under it. What was that thing? . . . I recognised my own floppy hat. It must have fallen off his head . . . and he didn't bother. Now I had what I wanted—the saving mark for my eyes. But I hardly thought of my other self, now gone from the ship, to be hidden for ever from all friendly faces, to be a fugitive and a vagabond on the earth, with no brand of the curse on his sane forehead to stay a slaying hand . . . too proud to explain.

And I watched the hat—the expression of my sudden pity for his mere flesh. It had been meant to save his homeless head from the dangers of the sun. And now —behold—it was saving the ship, by serving me for a mark to help out the ignorance of my strangeness. Ha! It was drifting forward, warning me just in time that the ship had gathered sternway.

"Shift the helm," I said in a low voice to the seaman standing still like a statue.

The man's eyes glistened wildly in the binnacle light

as he jumped round to the other side and spun round
the wheel.

I walked to the break of the poop. On the over-
shadowed deck all hands stood by the forebraces waiting for my order. The stars ahead seemed to be
gliding from right to left. And all was so still in the
world that I heard the quiet remark, "She's round,"
passed in a tone of intense relief between two seamen.

"Let go and haul."

The foreyards ran round with a great noise, amidst
cheery cries. And now the frightful whiskers made
themselves heard giving various orders. Already the
ship was drawing ahead. And I was alone with her.
Nothing! no one in the world should stand now between
us, throwing a shadow on the way of silent knowledge
and mute affection, the perfect communion of a seaman
with his first command.

Walking to the taffrail, I was in time to make out,
on the very edge of a darkness thrown by a towering
black mass like the very gateway of Erebus—yes, I was
in time to catch an evanescent glimpse of my white hat
left behind to mark the spot where the secret sharer of
my cabin and of my thoughts, as though he were my
second self, had lowered himself into the water to take
his punishment: a free man, a proud swimmer striking
out for a new destiny.

FREYA OF THE SEVEN ISLES

A STORY OF SHALLOW WATERS

FREYA OF THE SEVEN ISLES

I

ONE day—and that day was many years ago now—I received a long, chatty letter from one of my old chums and fellow-wanderers in Eastern waters. He was still out there, but settled down, and middle-aged; I imagined him grown portly in figure and domestic in his habits; in short, overtaken by the fate common to all except to those who, being specially beloved by the gods, get knocked on the head early. The letter was of the reminiscent "do you remember" kind—a wistful letter of backward glances. And, amongst other things, "surely you remember old Nelson," he wrote.

Remember old Nelson! Certainly. And to begin with, his name was not Nelson. The Englishmen in the Archipelago called him Nelson because it was more convenient, I suppose, and he never protested. It would have been mere pedantry. The true form of his name was Nielsen. He had come out East long before the advent of telegraph cables, had served English firms, had married an English girl, had been one of us for years, trading and sailing in all directions through the Eastern Archipelago, across and around, transversely, diagonally, perpendicularly, in semi-circles, and zigzags, and figures of eights, for years and years.

There was no nook or cranny of these tropical waters that the enterprise of old Nelson (or Nielsen) had not penetrated in an eminently pacific way. His tracks, if plotted out, would have covered the map of the Archipelago like a cobweb—all of it, with the sole exception of the Philippines. He would never approach that part, from a strange dread of Spaniards, or, to be exact, of the Spanish authorities. What he imagined they could do to him it is impossible to say. Perhaps at some time in his life he had read some stories of the Inquisition.

But he was in general afraid of what he called "authorities"; not the English authorities, which he trusted and respected, but the other two of that part of the world. He was not so horrified at the Dutch as he was at the Spaniards, but he was even more mistrustful of them. Very mistrustful indeed. The Dutch, in his view, were capable of "playing any ugly trick on a man" who had the misfortune to displease them. There were their laws and regulations, but they had no notion of fair play in applying them. It was really pitiable to see the anxious circumspection of his dealings with some official or other, and remember that this man had been known to stroll up to a village of cannibals in New Guinea in a quiet, fearless manner (and note that he was always fleshy all his life, and, if I may say so, an appetising morsel) on some matter of barter that did not amount perhaps to fifty pounds in the end.

Remember old Nelson! Rather! Truly, none of us in my generation had known him in his active days. He was "retired" in our time. He had bought, or else leased, part of a small island from the sultan of a little group called the Seven Isles, not far north from Banka. It was, I suppose, a legitimate transaction, but I have no doubt that had he been an Englishman the Dutch would have discovered a reason to fire him out without ceremony. In this connection the real form of his name stood him in good stead. In the character of an unassuming Dane whose conduct was most correct, they let him be. With all his money engaged in cultivation he was naturally careful not to give even the shadow of offence, and it was mostly for prudential reasons of that sort that he did not look with a favourable eye on Jasper Allen. But of that later. Yes! One remembered well enough old Nelson's big, hospitable bungalow erected on a shelving point of land, his portly form, costumed generally in a white shirt and trousers (he had a confirmed habit of taking off his alpaca jacket on the slightest provocation), his round blue eyes, his straggly, sandy-white moustache sticking out all ways like the quills of the fretful porcupine, his propensity to sit down suddenly and fan himself with his hat. But there's no use concealing the fact that what one remembered really was his daughter, who at that time came out to live with him —and be a sort of Lady of the Isles.

Freya Nelson (or Nielsen)was the kind of a girl one remembers. The oval of her face was perfect; and within that fascinating frame the most happy disposition of line and feature, with an admirable complexion, gave an impression of health, strength, and what I might call unconscious self-confidence—a most pleasant and, as it were, whimsical determination. I will not compare her eyes to violets, because the real shade of their colour was peculiar, not so dark and more lustrous. They were of the wide-open kind, and looked at one frankly in every mood. I never did see the long, dark eyelashes lowered—I dare say Jasper Allen did, being a privileged person—but I have no doubt that the expression must have been charming in a complex way. She could—Jasper told me once with a touchingly imbecile exultation—sit on her hair. I dare say, I dare say. It was not for me to behold these wonders; I was content to admire the neat and becoming way she used to do it up so as not to conceal the good shape of her head. And this wealth of hair was so glossy that when the screens of the west verandah were down, making a pleasant twilight there, or in the shade of the grove of fruit-trees near the house, it seemed to give out a golden light of its own.

She dressed generally in a white frock, with a skirt of walking length, showing her neat, laced, brown boots. If there was any colour about her costume it was just a bit of blue perhaps. No exertion seemed to distress her. I have seen her land from the dinghy after a long pull in the sun (she rowed herself about a good deal) with no quickened breath and not a single hair out of its place. In the morning when she came out on the verandah for the first look westward, Sumatra way, over the sea, she seemed as fresh and sparkling as a dewdrop. But a dewdrop is evanescent, and there was nothing evanescent about Freya. I remember her round, solid arms with the fine wrists, and her broad, capable hands with tapering fingers.

I don't know whether she was actually born at sea, but I do know that up to twelve years of age she sailed about with her parents in various ships. After old Nelson lost his wife it became a matter of serious concern for him what to do with the girl. A kind lady in Singapore, touched by his dumb grief and deplorable perplexity, offered to take charge of Freya. This arrangement lasted some six years, during which old Nelson (or Nielsen) "retired" and established himself on his island, and then it was settled (the kind lady going away to Europe) that his daughter should join him.

As the first and most important preparation for that

event the old fellow ordered from his Singapore agent a Steyn and Ebhart's "upright grand." I was then commanding a little steamer in the island trade, and it fell to my lot to take it out to him, so I know something of Freya's "upright grand." We landed the enormous packing-case with difficulty on a flat piece of rock amongst some bushes, nearly knocking the bottom out of one of my boats in the course of that nautical operation. Then, all my crew assisting, engineers and firemen included, by the exercise of much anxious ingenuity, and by means of rollers, levers, tackles, and inclined planes of soaped planks, toiling in the sun like ancient Egyptians at the building of a pyramid, we got it as far as the house and up on to the edge of the west verandah—which was the actual drawing-room of the bungalow. There, the case being ripped off cautiously, the beautiful rosewood monster stood revealed at last. In reverent excitement we coaxed it against the wall and drew the first free breath of the day. It was certainly the heaviest movable object on that islet since the creation of the world. The volume of sound it gave out in that bungalow (which acted as a sounding-board) was really astonishing. It thundered sweetly right over the sea. Jasper Allen told me that early of a morning on the deck of the *Bonito* (his wonderfully fast and pretty brig) he could hear Freya playing her scales quite distinctly. But the fellow always anchored foolishly close to the point, as I told him more than once. Of course, these seas are almost uniformly serene, and the Seven Isles is a particularly calm and cloudless spot as a rule. But still, now and again, an afternoon thunderstorm over Banka, or even one of these vicious thick squalls, from the distant Sumatra coast, would make a sudden sally upon the group, enveloping it for a couple of hours in whirlwinds and

bluish-black murk of a particularly sinister aspect.
Then, with the lowered rattan-screens rattling desperately in the wind and the bungalow shaking all over,
Freya would sit down to the piano and play fierce
Wagner music in the flicker of blinding flashes, with
thunderbolts falling all round, enough to make your
hair stand on end; and Jasper would remain stock still
on the verandah, adoring the back view of her supple,
swaying figure, the miraculous sheen of her fair head,
the rapid hands on the keys, the white nape of her
neck—while the brig, down at the point there, surged
at her cables within a hundred yards of nasty, shiny,
black rock-heads. Ugh!

And this, if you please, for no reason but that, when
he went on board at night and laid his head on the
pillow, he should feel that he was as near as he could
conveniently get to his Freya slumbering in the bungalow. Did you ever! And, mind, this brig was the
home to be—their home—the floating paradise which
he was gradually fitting out like a yacht to sail his life
blissfully away in with Freya. Imbecile! But the
fellow was always taking chances.

One day, I remember I watched with Freya on the
verandah the brig approaching the point from the
northward. I suppose Jasper made the girl out with
his long glass. What does he do? Instead of standing on for another mile and a half along the shoals and
then tacking for the anchorage in a proper and seaman-
like manner, he spies a gap between two disgusting old
jagged reefs, puts the helm down suddenly, and shoots
the brig through, with all her sails shaking and rattling,
so that we could hear the racket on the verandah. I
drew my breath through my teeth, I can tell you, and
Freya swore. Yes! She clenched her capable fists
and stamped with her pretty brown boot and said

"Damn!" Then, looking at me with a little heightened colour—not much—she remarked, "I forgot you were there," and laughed. To be sure, to be sure. When Jasper was in sight she was not likely to remember that anybody else in the world was there. In my concern at this mad trick I couldn't help appealing to her sympathetic common sense.

"Isn't he a fool?" I said with feeling.

"Perfect idiot," she agreed warmly, looking at me straight with her wide-open, earnest eyes and the dimple of a smile on her cheek.

"And that," I pointed out to her, "just to save twenty minutes or so in meeting you."

We heard the anchor go down, and then she became very resolute and threatening.

"Wait a bit. I'll teach him."

She went into her own room and shut the door, leaving me alone on the verandah with my instructions. Long before the brig's sails were furled, Jasper came up three steps at a time, forgetting to say how d'ye do, and looking right and left eagerly.

"Where's Freya? Wasn't she here just now?"

When I explained to him that he was to be deprived of Miss Freya's presence for a whole hour, "just to teach him," he said I had put her up to it, no doubt, and that he feared he would have yet to shoot me some day. She and I were getting too thick together. Then he flung himself into a chair, and tried to talk to me about his trip. But the funny thing was that the fellow actually suffered. I could see it. His voice failed him, and he sat there dumb, looking at the door with the face of a man in pain. Fact. . . . And the next still funnier thing was that the girl calmly walked out of her room in less than ten minutes. And then I left. I mean to say that I went away to seek old Nelson (or

Nielsen) on the back verandah, which was his own
special nook in the distribution of that house, with the
kind purpose of engaging him in conversation lest he
should start roaming about and intrude unwittingly
where he was not wanted just then.

He knew that the brig had arrived, though he did
not know that Jasper was already with his daughter.
I suppose he didn't think it was possible in the time.
A father naturally wouldn't. He suspected that Allen
was sweet on his girl; the fowls of the air and the fishes
of the sea, most of the traders in the Archipelago, and all
sorts and conditions of men in the town of Singapore
were aware of it. But he was not capable of appreciat-
ing how far the girl was gone on the fellow. He had an
idea that Freya was too sensible ever to be gone on anybody—I mean to an unmanageable extent. No; it was
not that which made him sit on the back verandah and
worry himself in his unassuming manner during Jasper's
visits. What he worried about were the Dutch "authorities." For it is a fact that the Dutch looked
askance at the doings of Jasper Allen, owner and master
of the brig *Bonito*. They considered him much too
enterprising in his trading. I don't know that he ever
did anything illegal; but it seems to me that his immense activity was repulsive to their stolid character
and slow-going methods. Anyway, in old Nelson's
opinion, the captain of the *Bonito* was a smart sailor,
and a nice young man, but not a desirable acquaintance
upon the whole. Somewhat compromising, you understand. On the other hand, he did not like to tell Jasper
in so many words to keep away. Poor old Nelson himself was a nice fellow. I believe he would have shrunk
from hurting the feelings even of a mop-headed cannibal,
unless, perhaps, under very strong provocation. I
mean the feelings, not the bodies. As against spears,

knives, hatchets, clubs, or arrows, old Nelson had proved himself capable of taking his own part. In every other respect he had a timorous soul. So he sat on the back verandah with a concerned expression, and whenever the voices of his daughter and Jasper Allen reached him, he would blow out his cheeks and let the air escape with a dismal sound, like a much tried man.

Naturally I derided his fears which he, more or less, confided to me. He had a certain regard for my judgment, and a certain respect, not for my moral qualities, however, but for the good terms I was supposed to be on with the Dutch "authorities." I knew for a fact that his greatest bugbear, the Governor of Banka—a charming, peppery, hearty, retired rear-admiral—had a distinct liking for him. This consoling assurance which I used always to put forward, made old Nelson (or Nielson) brighten up for a moment; but in the end he would shake his head doubtfully, as much as to say that this was all very well, but that there were depths in the Dutch official nature which no one but himself had ever fathomed. Perfectly ridiculous.

On this occasion I am speaking of, old Nelson was even fretty; for while I was trying to entertain him with a very funny and somewhat scandalous adventure which happened to a certain acquaintance of ours in Saigon, he exclaimed suddenly:

"What the devil he wants to turn up here for!"

Clearly he had not heard a word of the anecdote. And this annoyed me, because the anecdote was really good. I stared at him.

"Come, come!" I cried. "Don't you know what Jasper Allen is turning up here for?"

This was the first open allusion I had ever made to the true state of affairs between Jasper and his daughter. He took it very calmly.

"Oh, Freya is a sensible girl!" he murmured absently, his mind's eye obviously fixed on the "authorities." No; Freya was no fool. He was not concerned about that. He didn't mind it in the least. The fellow was just company for her; he amused the girl; nothing more.

When the perspicacious old chap left off mumbling, all was still in the house. The other two were amusing themselves very quietly, and no doubt very heartily. What more absorbing and less noisy amusement could they have found than to plan their future? Side by side on the verandah they must have been looking at the brig, the third party in that fascinating game. Without her there would have been no future. She was the fortune and the home, and the great free world for them. Who was it that likened a ship to a prison? May I be ignominiously hanged at a yardarm if that's true. The white sails of that craft were the white wings—pinions, I believe, would be the more poetical style—well, the white pinions, of their soaring love. Soaring as regards Jasper. Freya, being a woman, kept a better hold of the mundane connections of this affair.

But Jasper was elevated in the true sense of the word ever since the day when, after they had been gazing at the brig in one of those decisive silences that alone establish a perfect communion between creatures gifted with speech, he proposed that she should share the ownership of that treasure with him. Indeed, he presented the brig to her altogether. But then his heart was in the brig since the day he bought her in Manila from a certain middle-aged Peruvian, in a sober suit of black broadcloth, enigmatic and sententious, who, for all I know, might have stolen her on the South American coast, whence he said he had come over to the Philippines "for family reasons." This "for family reasons" was distinctly good. No true *caballero* would care to push on inquiries after such a statement.

Indeed, Jasper was quite the *caballero*. The brig herself was then all black and enigmatical, and very dirty; a tarnished gem of the sea, or, rather, a neglected work of art. For he must have been an artist, the obscure builder who had put her body together on lovely lines out of the hardest tropical timber fastened with the purest copper. Goodness only knows in what part of the world she was built. Jasper himself had not been able to ascertain much of her history from his sententious, saturnine Peruvian—if the fellow was a Peruvian, and not the devil himself in disguise, as Jasper jocularly pretended to believe. My opinion is that she was old enough to have been one of the last pirates, a slaver perhaps, or else an opium clipper of the early days, if not an opium smuggler.

However that may be, she was as sound as on the day she first took the water, sailed like a witch, steered like a little boat, and, like some fair women of adventurous life famous in history, seemed to have the secret of perpetual youth; so that there was nothing unnatural in Jasper Allen treating her like a lover. And that treatment restored the lustre of her beauty. He clothed her in many coats of the very best white paint so skilfully, carefully, artistically put on and kept clean by his badgered crew of picked Malays, that no costly enamel such as jewellers use for their work could have looked better and felt smoother to the touch. A narrow gilt moulding defined her elegant sheer as she sat on the water, eclipsing easily the professional good looks of any pleasure yacht that ever came to the East in those days. For myself, I must say I prefer a moulding of deep crimson colour on a white hull. It gives a stronger relief besides being less expensive; and I told Jasper so. But no, nothing less than the best gold-leaf would do, because no decoration could be gorgeous enough for the future abode of his Freya.

His feelings for the brig and for the girl were as indissolubly united in his heart as you may fuse two precious metals together in one crucible. And the flame was pretty hot, I can assure you. It induced in him a fierce inward restlessness both of activity and desire. Too fine in face, with a lateral wave in his chestnut hair, spare, long-limbed, with an eager glint in his steely eyes and quick, brusque movements, he made me think sometimes of a flashing sword-blade perpetually leaping out of the scabbard. It was only when he was near the girl, when he had her there to look at, that this peculiarly tense attitude was replaced by a grave devout watchfulness of her slightest movements and utterances. Her cool, resolute, capable, good-humoured self-possession seemed to steady his heart. Was it the magic of her face, of her voice, of her glances which calmed him so? Yet these were the very things one must believe which had set his imagination ablaze—if love begins in imagination. But I am no man to discuss such mysteries, and it strikes me that we have neglected poor old Nelson inflating his cheeks in a state of worry on the back verandah.

I pointed out to him that, after all, Jasper was not a very frequent visitor. He and his brig worked hard all over the Archipelago. But all old Nelson said, and he said it uneasily, was:

"I hope Heemskirk won't turn up here while the brig's about."

Getting up a scare about Heemskirk now! Heemskirk! . . . Really, one hadn't the patience——

II

FOR, pray, who was Heemskirk? You shall see at once how unreasonable this dread of Heemskirk. . . . Certainly, his nature was malevolent enough. That was obvious, directly you heard him laugh. Nothing gives away more a man's secret disposition than the unguarded ring of his laugh. But, bless my soul! if we were to start at every evil guffaw like a hare at every sound, we shouldn't be fit for anything but the solitude of a desert, or the seclusion of a hermitage. And even there we should have to put up with the unavoidable company of the devil.

However, the devil is a considerable personage, who has known better days and has moved high up in the hierarchy of Celestial Host; but in the hierarchy of mere earthly Dutchmen, Heemskirk, whose early days could not have been very splendid, was merely a naval officer forty years of age, of no particular connections or ability to boast of. He was commanding the *Neptun*, a little gunboat employed on dreary patrol duty up and down the Archipelago, to look after the traders. Not a very exalted position truly. I tell you, just a common middle-aged lieutenant of some twenty-five years' service and sure to be retired before long—that's all.

He never bothered his head very much as to what was going on in the Seven Isles group till he learned from some talk in Mintok or Palembang, I suppose, that there was a pretty girl living there. Curiosity, I presume, caused him to go poking around that way and then, after he had once seen Freya, he made a practice of calling at the group whenever he found himself within half a day's steaming from it.

I don't mean to say that Heemskirk was a typical Dutch naval officer. I have seen enough of them not to fall into that absurd mistake. He had a big, cleanshaven face; great flat, brown cheeks, with a thin, hooked nose and a small, pursy mouth squeezed in between. There were a few silver threads in his black hair, and his unpleasant eyes were nearly black, too. He had a surly way of casting side glances without moving his head, which was set low on a short, round neck. A thick, round trunk in a dark undress jacket with gold shoulder-straps, was sustained by a straddly pair of thick, round legs, in white drill trousers. His round skull under a white cap looked as if it were immensely thick too, but there were brains enough in it to discover and take advantage maliciously of poor old Nelson's nervousness before everything that was invested with the merest shred of authority.

Heemskirk would land on the point and perambulate silently every part of the plantation as if the whole place belonged to him, before he went to the house. On the verandah he would take the best chair, and would stay for tiffin or dinner, just simply stay on, without taking the trouble to invite himself by so much as a word.

He ought to have been kicked, if only for his manner to Miss Freya. Had he been a naked savage, armed with spears and poisoned arrows, old Nelson (or Nielsen) would have gone for him with his bare fists. But these gold shoulder-straps—Dutch shoulder-straps at that—were enough to terrify the old fellow; so he let the beggar treat him with heavy contempt, devour his daughter with his eyes, and drink the best part of his little stock of wine.

I saw something of this, and on one occasion I tried

to pass a remark on the subject. It was pitiable to see the trouble in old Nelson's round eyes. At first he cried out that the lieutenant was a good friend of his; a very good fellow. I went on staring at him pretty hard, so that at last he faltered, and had to own that, of course, Heemskirk was not a very genial person outwardly, but all the same at bottom. . . .

"I haven't yet met a genial Dutchman out here," I interrupted. "Geniality, after all, is not of much consequence, but don't you see——"

Nelson looked suddenly so frightened at what I was going to say that I hadn't the heart to go on. Of course, I was going to tell him that the fellow was after his girl. That just describes it exactly. What Heemskirk might have expected or what he thought he could do, I don't know. For all I can tell, he might have imagined himself irresistible, or have taken Freya for what she was not, on account of her lively, assured, unconstrained manner. But there it is. He was after that girl. Nelson could see it well enough. Only he preferred to ignore it. He did not want to be told of it.

"All I want is to live in peace and quietness with the Dutch authorities," he mumbled shamefacedly.

He was incurable. I was sorry for him, and I really think Miss Freya was sorry for her father, too. She restrained herself for his sake, and like everything she did she did it simply, unaffectedly, and even good humouredly. No small effort that, because in Heemskirk's attentions there was an insolent touch of scorn, hard to put up with. Dutchmen of that sort are overbearing to their inferiors, and that officer of the king looked upon old Nelson and Freya as quite beneath him in every way.

I can't say I felt sorry for Freya. She was not the

sort of girl to take anything tragically. One could feel for her and sympathise with her difficulty, but she seemed equal to any situation. It was rather admiration she extorted by her competent serenity. It was only when Jasper and Heemskirk were together at the bungalow, as it happened now and then, that she felt the strain, and even then it was not for everybody to see. My eyes alone could detect a faint shadow on the radiance of her personality. Once I could not help saying to her appreciatively:

"Upon my word you are wonderful."

She let it pass with a faint smile.

"The great thing is to prevent Jasper becoming unreasonable," she said; and I could see real concern lurking in the quiet depths of her frank eyes gazing straight at me. "You will help to keep him quiet, won't you?"

"Of course, we must keep him quiet," I declared, understanding very well the nature of her anxiety. "He's such a lunatic, too, when he's roused."

"He is!" she assented, in a soft tone; for it was our joke to speak of Jasper abusively. "But I have tamed him a bit. He's quite a good boy now."

"He would squash Heemskirk like a blackbeetle all the same," I remarked.

"Rather!" she murmured. "And that wouldn't do," she added quickly. "Imagine the state poor papa would get into. Besides, I mean to be mistress of the dear brig and sail about these seas, not go off wandering ten thousand miles away from here."

"The sooner you are on board to look after the man and the brig the better," I said seriously. "They need you to steady them both a bit. I don't think Jasper will ever get sobered down till he has carried you off from this island. You don't see him when he

is away from you, as I do.   He's in a state of perpetual
elation which almost frightens me."

At this she smiled again, and then looked serious.
For it could not be unpleasant to her to be told of
her power, and she had some sense of her responsibility.
She slipped away from me suddenly, because Heemskirk, with old Nelson in attendance at his elbow, was
coming up the steps of the verandah.   Directly his
head came above the level of the floor his ill-natured
black eyes shot glances here and there.

"Where's your girl, Nelson?" he asked, in a tone as
if every soul in the world belonged to him.   And then
to me: "The goddess has flown, eh?"

Nelson's Cove—as we used to call it—was crowded
with shipping that day.   There was first my steamer,
then the *Neptun* gunboat further out, and the *Bonito*,
brig, anchored as usual so close inshore that it looked as
if, with a little skill and judgment, one could shy a hat
from the verandah on to her scrupulously holystoned
quarter-deck.   Her brasses flashed like gold, her white
body-paint had a sheen like a satin robe.   The rake
of her varnished spars and the big yards, squared to a
hair, gave her a sort of martial elegance.   She was a
beauty.   No wonder that in possession of a craft like
that and the promise of a girl like Freya, Jasper lived in
a state of perpetual elation fit, perhaps, for the seventh
heaven, but not exactly safe in a world like ours.

I remarked politely to Heemskirk that, with three
guests in the house, Miss Freya had no doubt domestic
matters to attend to.   I knew, of course, that she had
gone to meet Jasper at a certain cleared spot on the
banks of the only stream on Nelson's little island.
The commander of the *Neptun* gave me a dubious black
look, and began to make himself at home, flinging his
thick, cylindrical carcass into a rocking-chair, and un-

buttoning his coat. Old Nelson sat down opposite him in a most unassuming manner, staring anxiously with his round eyes and fanning himself with his hat. I tried to make conversation to while the time away; not an easy task with a morose, enamoured Dutchman constantly looking from one door to another and answering one's advances either with a jeer or a grunt.

However, the evening passed off all right. Luckily there is a degree of bliss too intense for elation. Jasper was quiet and concentrated silently in watching Freya. As we went on board our respective ships I offered to give his brig a tow out next morning. I did it on purpose to get him away at the earliest possible moment. So in the first cold light of the dawn we passed by the gunboat lying black and still without a sound in her at the mouth of the glassy cove. But with tropical swiftness the sun had climbed twice its diameter above the horizon before we had rounded the reef and got abreast of the point. On the biggest boulder there stood Freya, all in white and, in her helmet, like a feminine and martial statue with a rosy face, as I could see very well with my glasses. She fluttered an expressive handkerchief, and Jasper, running up the main rigging of the white and warlike brig, waved his hat in response. Shortly afterwards we parted, I to the northward, and Jasper heading east with a light wind on the quarter, for Banjermassin and two other ports, I believe it was, that trip.

This peaceful occasion was the last on which I saw all these people assembled together; the charmingly fresh and resolute Freya, the innocently round-eyed old Nelson, Jasper, keen, long limbed, lean faced, admirably self-contained in his manner, because inconceivably happy under the eyes of his Freya; all three tall, fair, and blue-eyed in varied shades, and amongst them the swarthy, arrogant, black-haired Dutchman, shorter nearly by a head, and so much thicker than any of them that he seemed to be a creature capable of inflating itself, a grotesque specimen of mankind from some other planet.

The contrast struck me all at once as we stood in the lighted verandah, after rising from the dinner-table. I was fascinated by it for the rest of the evening, and I remember the impression of something funny and ill-omened at the same time in it to this day.

III

A FEW weeks later, coming early one morning into Singapore, from a journey to the southward, I saw the brig lying at anchor in all her usual symmetry and splendour of aspect as though she had been taken out of a glass case and put delicately into the water that very moment.

She was well out in the roadstead, but I steamed in and took up my habitual berth close in front of the town. Before we had finished breakfast a quartermaster came to tell me that Captain Allen's boat was coming our way.

His smart gig dashed alongside, and in two bounds he was up our accommodation-ladder and shaking me by the hand with his nervous grip, his eyes snapping inquisitively, for he supposed I had called at the Seven Isles group on my way. I reached into my pocket for a nicely folded little note, which he grabbed out of my hand without ceremony and carried off on the bridge to read by himself. After a decent interval I followed him up there, and found him pacing to and fro; for the nature of his emotions made him restless even in his most thoughtful moments.

He shook his head at me triumphantly.

"Well, my dear boy," he said, "I shall be counting the days now."

I understood what he meant. I knew that those young people had settled already on a runaway match without official preliminaries. This was really a logical decision. Old Nelson (or Nielsen) would never have agreed to give up Freya peaceably to this compromising Jasper. Heavens! What would the Dutch authorities say to such a match! It sounds too ridiculous for words. But there's nothing in the world more selfishly hard than a timorous man in a fright about his "little estate," as old Nelson used to call it in apologetic accents. A heart permeated by a particular sort of funk is proof against sense, feeling, and ridicule. It's a flint.

Jasper would have made his request all the same and then taken his own way; but it was Freya who decided that nothing should be said, on the ground that, "Papa would only worry himself to distraction." He was capable of making himself ill, and then she wouldn't have the heart to leave him. Here you have the sanity of feminine outlook and the frankness of feminine reasoning. And for the rest, Miss Freya could read "poor dear papa" in the way a woman reads a man—like an open book. His daughter once gone, old Nelson would not worry himself. He would raise a great outcry, and make no end of lamentable fuss, but that's not the same thing. The real agonies of indecision, the anguish of conflicting feelings would be spared to him. And as he was too unassuming to rage, he would, after a period of lamentation, devote himself to his "little estate," and to keeping on good terms with the authorities.

Time would do the rest. And Freya thought she

could afford to wait, while ruling over her own home in the beautiful brig and over the man who loved her. This was the life for her who had learned to walk on a ship's deck. She was a ship-child, a sea-girl if ever there was one. And of course she loved Jasper and trusted him; but there was a shade of anxiety in her pride. It is very fine and romantic to possess for your very own a finely tempered and trusty sword-blade, but whether it is the best weapon to counter with the common cudgel-play of Fate—that's another question.

She knew that she had the more substance of the two—you needn't try any cheap jokes, I am not talking of their weights. She was just a little anxious while he was away, and she had me who, being a tried confidant, took the liberty to whisper frequently "The sooner the better." But there was a peculiar vein of obstinacy in Miss Freya, and her reason for delay was characteristic. "Not before my twenty-first birthday; so that there shall be no mistake in people's minds as to me being old enough to know what I am doing."

Jasper's feelings were in such subjection that he had never even remonstrated against the decree. She was just splendid, whatever she did or said, and there was an end of it for him. I believe that he was subtle enough to be even flattered at bottom—at times. And then to console him he had the brig which seemed pervaded by the spirit of Freya, since whatever he did on board was always done under the supreme sanction of his love.

"Yes. I'll soon begin to count the days," he repeated. "Eleven months more. I'll have to crowd three trips into that."

"Mind you don't come to grief trying to do too much," I admonished him. But he dismissed my caution with a laugh and an elated gesture. Pooh!

Nothing, nothing could happen to the brig, he cried, as if the flame of his heart could light up the dark nights of uncharted seas, and the image of Freya serve for an unerring beacon amongst hidden shoals; as if the winds had to wait on his future, the stars fight for it in their courses; as if the magic of his passion had the power to float a ship on a drop of dew or sail her through the eye of a needle—simply because it was her magnificent lot to be the servant of a love so full of grace as to make all the ways of the earth safe, resplendent, and easy.

"I suppose," I said, after he had finished laughing at my innocent enough remark, "I suppose you will be off to-day."

That was what he meant to do. He had not gone at daylight only because he expected me to come in.

"And only fancy what has happened yesterday," he went on. "My mate left me suddenly. Had to. And as there's nobody to be found at a short notice I am going to take Schultz with me. The notorious Schultz! Why don't you jump out of your skin? I tell you I went and unearthed Schultz late last evening, after no end of trouble. 'I am your man, Captain,' he says, in that wonderful voice of his, 'but I am sorry to confess I have practically no clothes to my back. I have had to sell all my wardrobe to get a little food from day to day.' What a voice that man has got. Talk about moving stones! But people seem to get used to it. I had never seen him before, and, upon my word, I felt suddenly tears rising to my eyes. Luckily it was dusk. He was sitting very quiet under a tree in a native compound as thin as a lath, and when I peered down at him all he had on was an old cotton singlet and a pair of ragged pyjamas. I bought him six white suits and two pairs of canvas shoes. Can't clear the ship without a mate. Must have somebody. I am going on shore presently to sign him on, and I shall take him with me as I go back on board to get under way. Now, I am a lunatic—am I not? Mad, of course. Come on! Lay it on thick. Let yourself go. I like to see you get excited."

He so evidently expected me to scold that I took especial pleasure in exaggerating the calmness of my attitude.

"The worst that can be brought up against Schultz," I began, folding my arms and speaking dispassionately, "is an awkward habit of stealing the stores of every ship he has ever been in. He will do it. That's really all that's wrong. I don't credit absolutely that story Captain Robinson tells of Schultz conspiring in Chantabun with some ruffians in a Chinese junk to steal the anchor off the starboard bow of the *Bohemian Girl* schooner. Robinson's story is too ingenious altogether. That other tale of the engineers of the *Nan-Shan* finding Schultz at midnight in the engine-room busy hammering at the brass bearings to carry them off for sale on shore seems to me more authentic. Apart from this little weakness, let me tell you that Schultz is a smarter sailor than many who never took a drop of drink in their lives, and perhaps no worse morally than some men you and I know who have never stolen the value of a penny. He may not be a desirable person to have on board one's ship, but since you have no choice he may be made to do, I believe. The important thing is to understand his psychology. Don't give him any money till you have done with him. Not a cent, if he begs you ever so. For as sure as Fate the moment you give him any money he will begin to steal. Just remember that."

I enjoyed Jasper's incredulous surprise.

"The devil he will!" he cried. "What on earth for? Aren't you trying to pull my leg, old boy?"

"No. I'm not. You must understand Schultz's psychology. He's neither a loafer nor a cadger. He's not likely to wander about looking for somebody to stand him drinks. But suppose he goes on shore with five dollars, or fifty for that matter, in his pocket? After the third or fourth glass he becomes fuddled and charitable. He either drops his money all over the place, or else distributes the lot around; gives it to any one who will take it. Then it occurs to him that the night is young yet, and that he may require a good many more drinks for himself and his friends before morning. So he starts off cheerfully for his ship. His legs never get affected nor his head either in the usual way. He gets aboard and simply grabs the first thing that seems to him suitable—the cabin lamp, a coil of rope, a bag of biscuits, a drum of oil—and converts it into money without thinking twice about it. This is the process and no other. You have only to look out that he doesn't get a start. That's all."

"Confound his psychology," muttered Jasper. "But a man with a voice like his is fit to talk to the angels. Is he incurable do you think?"

I said that I thought so. Nobody had prosecuted him yet, but no one would employ him any longer. His end would be, I feared, to starve in some hole or other.

"Ah, well," reflected Jasper. "The *Bonito* isn't trading to any ports of civilisation. That'll make it easier for him to keep straight."

That was true. The brig's business was on uncivilised coasts, with obscure rajahs dwelling in nearly unknown bays; with native settlements up mysterious rivers opening their sombre, forest-lined estuaries

among a welter of pale green reefs and dazzling sand-
banks, in lonely straits of calm blue water all aglitter
with sunshine. Alone, far from the beaten tracks, she
glided, all white, round dark, frowning headlands, stole
out, silent like a ghost, from behind points of land
stretching out all black in the moonlight; or lay hove-to,
like a sleeping sea-bird, under the shadow of some
nameless mountain waiting for a signal. She would
be glimpsed suddenly on misty, squally days dashing
disdainfully aside the short aggressive waves of the
Java Sea; or be seen far, far away, a tiny dazzling
white speck flying across the brooding purple masses
of thunderclouds piled up on the horizon. Sometimes,
on the rare mail tracks, where civilisation brushes
against wild mystery, when the naïve passengers crowd-
ing along the rail exclaimed, pointing at her with
interest: "Oh, here's a yacht!" the Dutch captain,
with a hostile glance, would grunt contemptuously:
"Yacht! No! That's only English Jasper. A ped-
lar——"

"A good seaman you say," ejaculated Jasper, still
in the matter of the hopeless Schultz with the wonderfully touching voice.

"First rate. Ask any one. Quite worth having—
only impossible," I declared.

"He shall have his chance to reform in the brig," said
Jasper, with a laugh. "There will be no temptations
either to drink or steal where I am going to this time."

I didn't press him for anything more definite on that
point. In fact, intimate as we were, I had a pretty
clear notion of the general run of his business.

But as we are going ashore in his gig he asked suddenly: "By the way, do you know where Heemskirk
is?"

I eyed him covertly, and was reassured. He had

asked the question, not as a lover, but as a trader. I told him that I had heard in Palembang that the *Neptun* was on duty down about Flores and Sumbawa. Quite out of his way. He expressed his satisfaction.

"You know," he went on, "that fellow, when he gets on the Borneo coast, amuses himself by knocking down my beacons. I have had to put up a few to help me in and out of the rivers. Early this year a Celebes trader becalmed in a prau was watching him at it. He steamed the gunboat full tilt at two of them, one after another, smashing them to pieces, and then lowered a boat on purpose to pull out a third, which I had a lot of trouble six months ago to stick up in the middle of a mudflat for a tide mark. Did you ever hear of anything more provoking—eh?"

"I wouldn't quarrel with the beggar," I observed casually, yet disliking that piece of news strongly. "It isn't worth while."

"I quarrel?" cried Jasper. "I don't want to quarrel. I don't want to hurt a single hair of his ugly head. My dear fellow, when I think of Freya's twenty-first birthday, all the world's my friend, Heemskirk included. It's a nasty, spiteful amusement, all the same."

We parted rather hurriedly on the quay, each of us having his own pressing business to attend to. I would have been very much cut up had I known that this hurried grasp of the hand with "So long, old boy. Good luck to you!" was the last of our partings.

On his return to the Straits I was away, and he was gone again before I got back. He was trying to achieve three trips before Freya's twenty-first birthday. At Nelson's Cove I missed him again by only a couple of days. Freya and I talked of "that lunatic" and "perfect idiot" with great delight and infinite appreciation. She was very radiant, with a more pronounced gaiety, notwithstanding that she had just parted from Jasper. But this was to be their last separation.

"Do get aboard as soon as you can, Miss Freya," I entreated.

She looked me straight in the face, her colour a little heightened and with a sort of solemn ardour—if there was a little catch in her voice.

"The very next day."

Ah, yes! The very next day after her twenty-first birthday. I was pleased at this hint of deep feeling. It was as if she had grown impatient at last of the self-imposed delay. I supposed that Jasper's recent visit had told heavily.

"That's right," I said approvingly. "I shall be much easier in my mind when I know you have taken charge of that lunatic. Don't you lose a minute. He, of course, will be on time—unless heavens fall."

"Yes. Unless——" she repeated in a thoughtful whisper, raising her eyes to the evening sky without a speck of cloud anywhere. Silent for a time, we let our eyes wander over the waters below, looking mysteriously still in the twilight, as if trustfully composed for a long, long dream in the warm, tropical night. And the peace all round us seemed without limits and without end.

And then we began to talk Jasper over in our usual strain. We agreed that he was too reckless in many ways. Luckily, the brig was equal to the situation. Nothing apparently was too much for her. A perfect darling of a ship, said Miss Freya. She and her father had spent an afternoon on board. Jasper had given them some tea. Papa was grumpy. . . . I had a vision of old Nelson under the brig's snowy awnings, nursing his unassuming vexation, and fanning himself with his hat. A comedy father. . . . As a new instance of Jasper's lunacy, I was told that he was distressed at his inability to have solid silver handles fitted to all the cabin doors. "As if I would have let him!" commented Miss Freya, with amused indignation. Incidentally, I learned also that Schultz, the nautical kleptomaniac with the pathetic voice, was still hanging on to his job, with Miss Freya's approval. Jasper had confided to the lady of his heart his purpose of straightening out the fellow's psychology. Yes, indeed. All the world was his friend because it breathed the same air with Freya.

Somehow or other, I brought Heemskirk's name into conversation, and, to my great surprise, startled Miss Freya. Her eyes expressed something like distress, while she bit her lip as if to contain an explosion of laughter. Oh! Yes. Heemskirk was at the bungalow at the same time with Jasper, but he arrived the day after. He left the same day as the brig, but a few hours later.

"What a nuisance he must have been to you two," I said feelingly.

Her eyes flashed at me a sort of frightened merriment, and suddenly she exploded into a clear burst of laughter. "Ha, ha, ha!"

I echoed it heartily, but not with the same charming tone: "Ha, ha, ha! . . . Isn't he grotesque? Ha, ha, ha!" And the ludicrousness of old Nelson's inanely fierce round eyes in association with his conciliatory manner to the lieutenant presenting itself to my mind brought on another fit.

"He looks," I spluttered, "he looks—Ha, ha, ha! —amongst you three . . . like an unhappy black-beetle. Ha, ha, ha!"

She gave out another ringing peal, ran off into her own room, and slammed the door behind her, leaving me profoundly astounded. I stopped laughing at once.

"What's the joke?" asked old Nelson's voice, half way down the steps.

He came up, sat down, and blew out his cheeks, looking inexpressibly fatuous. But I didn't want to laugh any more. "And what on earth," I asked myself, "have we been laughing at in this uncontrollable fashion?" I felt suddenly depressed.

Oh, yes. Freya had started it. The girl's over-wrought, I thought. And really one couldn't wonder at it.

I had no answer to old Nelson's question, but he was too aggrieved at Jasper's visit to think of anything else. He as good as asked me whether I wouldn't undertake to hint to Jasper that he was not wanted at the Seven Isles group. I declared that it was not necessary. From certain circumstances which had come to my knowledge lately, I had reason to think that he would not be much troubled by Jasper Allen in the future.

He emitted an earnest "Thank God!" which nearly set me laughing again, but he did not brighten up proportionately. It seemed Heemskirk had taken special pains to make himself disagreeable. The lieutenant had frightened old Nelson very much by expressing a sinister wonder at the Government permitting a white man to settle down in that part at all. "It is against our declared policy," he had remarked. He had also charged him with being in reality no better than an Englishman. He had even tried to pick a quarrel with him for not learning to speak Dutch.

"I told him I was too old to learn now," sighed out old Nelson (or Nielsen) dismally. "He said I ought to have learned Dutch long before. I had been making my living in Dutch dependencies. It was disgraceful of me not to speak Dutch, he said. He was as savage with me as if I had been a Chinaman."

It was plain he had been viciously badgered. He did not mention how many bottles of his best claret he had offered up on the altar of conciliation. It must have been a generous libation. But old Nelson (or Nielsen) was really hospitable. He didn't mind that; and I only regretted that this virtue should be lavished on the lieutenant-commander of the *Neptun*. I longed to tell him that in all probability he would be relieved from Heemskirk's visitations also. I did not do so only from the fear (absurd, I admit) of arousing some sort of suspicion in his mind. As if with this guileless comedy father such a thing were possible!

Strangely enough, the last words on the subject of Heemskirk were spoken by Freya, and in that very sense. The lieutenant was turning up persistently in old Nelson's conversation at dinner. At last I muttered a half audible, "Damn the lieutenant." I could see that the girl was getting exasperated, too.

"And he wasn't well at all—was he, Freya?" old Nelson went on moaning. "Perhaps it was that which made him so snappish, hey, Freya? He looked very bad when he left us so suddenly. His liver must be in a bad state, too."

"Oh, he will end by getting over it," said Freya impatiently. "And do leave off worrying about him, papa. Very likely you won't see much of him for a long time to come."

The look she gave me in exchange for my discreet smile had no hidden mirth in it. Her eyes seemed hollowed, her face gone wan in a couple of hours. We had been laughing too much. Overwrought! Overwrought by the approach of the decisive moment. After all, sincere, courageous, and self-reliant as she

was, she must have felt both the passion and the compunction of her resolve. The very strength of love
which had carried her up to that point must have put
her under a great moral strain, in which there might
have been a little simple remorse, too. For she was
honest—and there, across the table, sat poor old
Nelson (or Nielsen) staring at her, round-eyed and so
pathetically comic in his fierce aspect as to touch the
most lightsome heart.

He retired early to his room to soothe himself for a
night's rest by perusing his account-books. We two
remained on the verandah for another hour or so, but
we exchanged only languid phrases on things without
importance, as though we had been emotionally jaded
by our long day's talk on the only momentous subject.
And yet there was something she might have told a
friend. But she didn't. We parted silently. She
distrusted my masculine lack of common sense, perhaps. . . . O Freya!

Going down the precipitous path to the landing-
stage, I was confronted in the shadows of boulders and
bushes by a draped feminine figure whose appearance
startled me at first. It glided into my way suddenly
from behind a piece of rock. But in a moment
it occurred to me that it could be no one else
but Freya's maid, a half-caste Malacca Portuguese.
One caught fleeting glimpses of her olive face and
dazzling white teeth about the house. I had also
observed her at times from a distance, as she sat within
call under the shade of some fruit-trees, brushing and
plaiting her long raven locks. It seemed to be the
principal occupation of her leisure hours. We had
often exchanged nods and smiles—and a few words,
too. She was a pretty creature. And once I had
watched her approvingly make funny and expressive

grimaces behind Heemskirk's back. I understood (from Jasper) that she was in the secret, like a comedy camerista. She was to accompany Freya on her irregular way to matrimony and "ever after" happiness. "Why should she be roaming by night near the cove— unless on some love affair of her own?" I asked myself. But there was nobody suitable within the Seven Isles group, as far as I knew. It flashed upon me that it was myself she had been lying in wait for.

She hesitated, muffled from head to foot, shadowy and bashful. I advanced another pace, and how I felt is nobody's business.

"What is it?" I asked, very low.

"Nobody knows I am here," she whispered.

"And nobody can see us," I whispered back.

The murmur of words "I've been so frightened" reached me. Just then forty feet above our head, from the yet lighted verandah, unexpected and startling, Freya's voice rang out in a clear, imperious call:

"Antonia!"

With a stifled exclamation, the hesitating girl vanished out of the path. A bush near by rustled; then silence. I waited wondering. The lights on the verandah went out. I waited a while longer then continued down the path to my boat, wondering more than ever.

I remember the occurrences of that visit especially, because this was the last time I saw the Nelson bungalow. On arriving at the Straits I found cable messages which made it necessary for me to throw up my employment at a moment's notice and go home at once. I had a desperate scramble to catch the mailboat which was due to leave next day, but I found time to write two short notes, one to Freya, the other to Jasper. Later on I wrote at length, this time to Allen alone. I got no answer. I hunted up then his brother, or, rather, half-brother, a solicitor in the city, a sallow, calm, little man who looked at me over his spectacles thoughtfully.

Jasper was the only child of his father's second marriage, a transaction which had failed to commend itself to the first, grown-up family.

"You haven't heard for ages," I repeated, with secret annoyance. "May I ask what 'for ages' means in this connection?"

"It means that I don't care whether I ever hear from him or not," retorted the little man of law, turning nasty suddenly.

I could not blame Jasper for not wasting his time in correspondence with such an outrageous relative. But why didn't he write to me—a decent sort of friend, after all; enough of a friend to find for his silence the excuse of forgetfulness natural to a state of transcendental bliss? I waited indulgently, but nothing ever came. And the East seemed to drop out of my life without an echo, like a stone falling into a well of prodigious depth.

IV

I SUPPOSE praiseworthy motives are a sufficient justification almost for anything. What could be more commendable in the abstract than a girl's determination that "poor papa" should not be worried, and her anxiety that the man of her choice should be kept by any means from every occasion of doing something rash, something which might endanger the whole scheme of their happiness?

Nothing could be more tender and more prudent. We must also remember the girl's self-reliant tempera-

ment, and the general unwillingness of women—I mean
women of sense—to make a fuss over matters of that
sort.

As has been said already, Heemskirk turned up some
time after Jasper's arrival at Nelson's Cove. The sight
of the brig lying right under the bungalow was very
offensive to him. He did not fly ashore before his
anchor touched the ground as Jasper used to do. On
the contrary, he hung about his quarter-deck mumbling
to himself; and when he ordered his boat to be manned
it was in an angry voice. Freya's existence, which
lifted Jasper out of himself into a blissful elation, was for
Heemskirk a cause of secret torment, of hours of exasperated brooding.

While passing the brig he hailed her harshly and
asked if the master was on board. Schultz, smart and
neat in a spotless white suit, leaned over the taffrail,
finding the question somewhat amusing. He looked
humorously down into Heemskirk's boat, and answered,
in the most amiable modulations of his beautiful voice:
"Captain Allen is up at the house, sir." But his expression changed suddenly at the savage growl: "What
the devil are you grinning at?" which acknowledged
that information.

He watched Heemskirk land and, instead of going
to the house, stride away by another path into the
grounds.

The desire-tormented Dutchman found old Nelson
(or Nielsen) at his drying-sheds, very busy superintend-
ing the manipulation of his tobacco crop, which, though
small, was of excellent quality, and enjoying himself
thoroughly. But Heemskirk soon put a stop to this
simple happiness. He sat down by the old chap, and
by the sort of talk which he knew was best calculated
for the purpose, reduced him before long to a state of

concealed and perspiring nervousness. It was a horrid talk of "authorities," and old Nelson tried to defend himself. If he dealt with English traders it was because he had to dispose of his produce somehow. He was as conciliatory as he knew how to be, and this very thing seemed to excite Heemskirk, who had worked himself up into a heavily breathing state of passion.

"And the worst of them all is that Allen," he growled. "Your particular friend—eh? You have let in a lot of these Englishmen into this part. You ought never to have been allowed to settle here. Never. What's he doing here now?"

Old Nelson (or Nielsen), becoming very agitated, declared that Jasper Allen was no particular friend of his. No friend at all—at all. He had bought three tons of rice from him to feed his workpeople on. What sort of evidence of friendship was that? Heemskirk burst out at last with the thought that had been gnawing at his vitals:

"Yes. Sell three tons of rice and flirt three days with that girl of yours. I am speaking to you as a friend, Nielsen. This won't do. You are only on sufferance here."

Old Nelson was taken aback at first, but recovered pretty quickly. Won't do! Certainly! Of course, it wouldn't do! The last man in the world. But his girl didn't care for the fellow, and was too sensible to fall in love with any one. He was very earnest in impressing on Heemskirk his own feeling of absolute security. And the lieutenant, casting doubting glances sideways, was yet willing to believe him.

"Much you know about it," he grunted nevertheless.

"But I do know," insisted old Nelson, with the greater desperation because he wanted to resist the doubts arising in his own mind. "My own daughter! In my own house, and I not to know! Come! It would be a good joke, lieutenant."

"They seem to be carrying on considerably," remarked Heemskirk moodily. "I suppose they are together now," he added, feeling a pang which changed what he meant for a mocking smile into a strange grimace.

The harassed Nelson shook his hand at him. He was at bottom shocked at this insistence, and was even beginning to feel annoyed at the absurdity of it.

"Pooh! Pooh! I'll tell you what, lieutenant: you go to the house and have a drop of gin-and-bitters before dinner. Ask for Freya. I must see the last of this tobacco put away for the night, but I'll be along presently."

Heemskirk was not insensible to this suggestion. It answered to his secret longing, which was not a longing for drink, however. Old Nelson shouted solicitously after his broad back a recommendation to make himself comfortable, and that there was a box of cheroots on the verandah.

It was the west verandah that old Nelson meant, the one which was the living-room of the house, and had split-rattan screens of the very finest quality. The east verandah, sacred to his own privacy, puffing out of cheeks, and other signs of perplexed thinking, was fitted with stout blinds of sailcloth. The north verandah was not a verandah at all, really. It was more like a long balcony. It did not communicate with the other two, and could only be approached by a passage inside the house. Thus it had a privacy which made it a convenient place for a maiden's meditations without words, and also for the discourses, apparently without sense, which, passing between a young man and a maid, become pregnant with a diversity of transcendental meanings.

This north verandah was embowered with climbing plants. Freya, whose room opened out on it, had furnished it as a sort of boudoir for herself, with a few cane chairs and a sofa of the same kind. On this sofa she and Jasper sat as close together as is possible in this imperfect world where neither can a body be in two places at once nor yet two bodies can be in one place at the same time. They had been sitting together all the afternoon, and I won't say that their talk had been without sense. Loving him with a little judicious anxiety lest in his elation he should break his heart over some mishap, Freya naturally would talk to him soberly. He, nervous and brusque when away from her, appeared always as if overcome by her visibility, by the great wonder of being palpably loved. An old man's child, having lost his mother early, thrown out to sea out of the way while very young, he had not much experience of tenderness of any kind.

In this private, foliage-embowered verandah, and at this late hour of the afternoon, he bent down a little, and, possessing himself of Freya's hands, was kissing them one after another, while she smiled and looked down at his head with the eyes of approving compassion. At that same moment Heemskirk was approaching the house from the north.

Antonia was on the watch on that side. But she did not keep a very good watch. The sun was setting; she knew that her young mistress and the captain of the *Bonito* were about to separate. She was walking to and fro in the dusky grove with a flower in her hair, and singing softly to herself, when suddenly, within a foot of her, the lieutenant appeared from behind a tree. She bounded aside like a startled fawn, but Heemskirk, with a lucid comprehension of what she was there for, pounced upon her, and, catching her arm, clapped his other thick hand over her mouth.

"If you try to make a noise I'll twist your neck!"

This ferocious figure of speech terrified the girl sufficiently. Heemskirk had seen plainly enough on the verandah Freya's golden head with another head very close to it. He dragged the unresisting maid with him by a circuitous way into the compound, where he dismissed her with a vicious push in the direction of the cluster of bamboo huts for the servants.

She was very much like the faithful camerista of Italian comedy, but in her terror she bolted away without a sound from that thick, short, black-eyed man with a cruel grip of fingers like a vice. Quaking all over at a distance, extremely scared and half inclined to laugh, she saw him enter the house at the back.

The interior of the bungalow was divided by two passages crossing each other in the middle. At that point Heemskirk by turning his head slightly to the left as he passed, secured the evidence of "carrying on" so irreconcilable with old Nelson's assurances that it made him stagger, with a rush of blood to his head. Two white figures, distinct against the light, stood in an unmistakable attitude. Freya's arms were round Jasper's neck. Their faces were characteristically superimposed on each other, and Heemskirk went on, his throat choked with a sudden rising of curses, till on the west verandah he stumbled blindly against a chair and then dropped into another as though his legs had been swept from under him. He had indulged too long in the habit of appropriating Freya to himself in his thoughts. "Is that how you entertain your visitors—you . . ." he thought, so outraged that he could not find a sufficiently degrading epithet.

Freya struggled a little and threw her head back. "Somebody has come in," she whispered. Jasper, holding her clasped closely to his breast, and looking down into her face, suggested casually:

"Your father."

Freya tried to disengage herself, but she had not the heart absolutely to push him away with her hands.

"I believe it's Heemskirk," she breathed out at him.

He, plunging into her eyes in a quiet rapture, was provoked to a vague smile by the sound of the name.

"The ass is always knocking down my beacons outside the river," he murmured. He attached no other meaning to Heemskirk's existence; but Freya was asking herself whether the lieutenant had seen them.

"Let me go, kid," she ordered in a peremptory whisper. Jasper obeyed, and, stepping back at once, continued his contemplation of her face under another angle. "I must go and see," she said to herself anxiously.

She instructed him hurriedly to wait a moment after she was gone and then to slip on to the back verandah and get a quiet smoke before he showed himself.

"Don't stay late this evening," was her last recommendation before she left him.

Then Freya came out on the west verandah with her light, rapid step. While going through the doorway she managed to shake down the folds of the looped-up curtains at the end of the passage so as to cover Jasper's retreat from the bower. Directly she appeared Heemskirk jumped up as if to fly at her. She paused and he made her an exaggerated low bow.

It irritated Freya.

"Oh! It's you, Mr. Heemskirk. How do you do?"

She spoke in her usual tone. Her face was not

plainly visible to him in the dusk of the deep verandah. He dared not trust himself to speak, his rage at what he had seen was so great. And when she added with serenity: "Papa will be coming in before long," he called her horrid names silently, to himself, before he spoke with contorted lips.

"I have seen your father already. We had a talk in the sheds. He told me some very interesting things. Oh, very——"

Freya sat down. She thought: "He has seen us, for certain." She was not ashamed. What she was afraid of was some foolish or awkward complication. But she could not conceive how much her person had been appropriated by Heemskirk (in his thoughts). She tried to be conversational.

"You are coming now from Palembang, I suppose?"

"Eh? What? Oh, yes! I come from Palembang. Ha, ha, ha! You know what your father said? He said he was afraid you were having a very dull time of it here."

"And I suppose you are going to cruise in the Moluccas," continued Freya, who wanted to impart some useful information to Jasper if possible. At the same time she was always glad to know that those two men were a few hundred miles apart when not under her eye.

Heemskirk growled angrily.

"Yes. Moluccas," glaring in the direction of her shadowy figure. "Your father thinks it's very quiet for you here. I tell you what, Miss Freya. There isn't such a quiet spot on earth that a woman can't find an opportunity of making a fool of somebody."

Freya thought: "I mustn't let him provoke me." Presently the Tamil boy, who was Nelson's head servant, came in with the lights. She addressed him at once with voluble directions where to put the lamps,

told him to bring the tray with the gin-and-bitters, and
to send Antonia into the house.

"I will have to leave you to yourself, Mr. Heemskirk, for a while," she said.

And she went to her room to put on another frock.
She made a quick change of it because she wished to
be on the verandah before her father and the lieutenant
met again. She relied on herself to regulate that
evening's intercourse between these two. But Antonia,
still scared and hysterical, exhibited a bruise on her
arm which roused Freya's indignation.

"He jumped on me out of the bush like a tiger,"
said the girl, laughing nervously with frightened eyes.

"The brute!" thought Freya. "He meant to spy
on us, then." She was enraged, but the recollection
of the thick Dutchman in white trousers wide at the
hips and narrow at the ankles, with his shoulder-straps
and black bullet head, glaring at her in the light of the
lamps, was so repulsively comical that she could not
help a smiling grimace. Then she became anxious.
The absurdities of three men were forcing this anxiety
upon her: Jasper's impetuosity, her father's fears,
Heemskirk's infatuation. She was very tender to the
first two, and she made up her mind to display all her
feminine diplomacy. All this, she said to herself, will
be over and done with before very long now.

Heemskirk on the verandah, lolling in a chair, his
legs extended and his white cap reposing on his stomach,
was lashing himself into a fury of an atrocious character
altogether incomprehensible to a girl like Freya. His
chin was resting on his chest, his eyes gazed stonily
at his shoes. Freya examined him from behind the
curtain. He didn't stir. He was ridiculous. But this
absolute stillness was impressive. She stole back along
the passage to the east verandah, where Jasper was

sitting quietly in the dark, doing what he was told, like a good boy.

"Psst," she hissed. He was by her side in a moment.

"Yes. What is it?" he murmured.

"It's that beetle," she whispered uneasily. Under the impression of Heemskirk's sinister immobility she had half a mind to let Jasper know that they had been seen. But she was by no means certain that Heemskirk would tell her father—and at any rate not that evening. She concluded rapidly that the safest thing would be to get Jasper out of the way as soon as possible.

"What has he been doing?" asked Jasper in a calm undertone.

"Oh, nothing! Nothing. He sits there looking cross. But you know how he's always worrying papa."

"Your father's quite unreasonable," pronounced Jasper judicially.

"I don't know," she said in a doubtful tone. Something of old Nelson's dread of the authorities had rubbed off on the girl since she had to live with it day after day. "I don't know. Papa's afraid of being reduced to beggary, as he says, in his old days. Look here, kid, you had better clear out to-morrow, first thing."

Jasper had hoped for another afternoon with Freya, an afternoon of quiet felicity with the girl by his side and his eyes on his brig, anticipating a blissful future. His silence was eloquent with disappointment, and Freya understood it very well. She, too, was disappointed. But it was her business to be sensible.

"We shan't have a moment to ourselves with that beetle creeping round the house," she argued in a low, hurried voice. "So what's the good of your staying?

And he won't go while the brig's here. You know he won't."

"He ought to be reported for loitering," murmured Jasper with a vexed little laugh.

"Mind you get under way at daylight," recommended Freya under her breath.

He detained her after the manner of lovers. She expostulated without struggling because it was hard for her to repulse him. He whispered into her ear while he put his arms round her.

"Next time we two meet, next time I hold you like this, it shall be on board. You and I, in the brig— all the world, all the life——" And then he flashed out: "I wonder I can wait! I feel as if I must carry you off now, at once. I could run with you in my hands—down the path—without stumbling—without touching the earth——"

She was still. She listened to the passion in his voice. She was saying to herself that if she were to whisper the faintest yes, if she were but to sigh lightly her consent, he would do it. He was capable of doing it—without touching the earth. She closed her eyes and smiled in the dark, abandoning herself in a delightful giddiness, for an instant, to his encircling arm. But before he could be tempted to tighten his grasp she was out of it, a foot away from him and in full possession of herself.

That was the steady Freya. She was touched by the deep sigh which floated up to her from the white figure of Jasper, who did not stir.

"You are a mad kid," she said tremulously. Then with a change of tone: "No one could carry me off. Not even you. I am not the sort of girl that gets carried off." His white form seemed to shrink a little before the force of that assertion and she relented. "Isn't it enough for you to know that you have—that you have carried me away?" she added in a tender tone.

He murmured an endearing word, and she continued: "I've promised you—I've said I would come—and I shall come of my own free will. You shall wait for me on board. I shall get up the side—by myself, and walk up to you on the deck and say: 'Here I am, kid.' And then—and then I shall be carried off. But it will be no man who will carry me off—it will be the brig, your brig—our brig. . . . I love the beauty!"

She heard an inarticulate sound, something like a moan wrung out by pain or delight, and glided away. There was that other man on the other verandah, that dark, surly Dutchman who could make trouble between Jasper and her father, bring about a quarrel, ugly words, and perhaps a physical collision. What a horrible situation! But, even putting aside that awful extremity, she shrank from having to live for some three months with a wretched, tormented, angry, distracted, absurd man. And when the day came, the day and the hour, what should she do if her father tried to detain her by main force—as was, after all, possible? Could she actually struggle with him hand to hand? But it was of lamentations and entreaties that she was really afraid. Could she withstand them? What an odious, cruel, ridiculous position would that be!

"But it won't be. He'll say nothing," she thought as she came out quickly on the west verandah, and, seeing that Heemskirk did not move, sat down on a chair near the doorway and kept her eyes on him. The outraged lieutenant had not changed his attitude; only his cap had fallen off his stomach and was lying on the floor. His thick black eyebrows were knitted by a frown, while he looked at her out of the corners of his eyes. And their sideways glance in conjunction with the hooked nose, the whole bulky, ungainly, sprawling person, struck Freya as so comically moody that, inwardly discomposed as she was, she could not help smiling. She did her best to give that smile a conciliatory character. She did not want to provoke Heemskirk needlessly.

And the lieutenant, perceiving that smile, was mollified. It never entered his head that his outward appearance, a naval officer, in uniform, could appear ridiculous to that girl of no position—the daughter of old Nielsen. The recollection of her arms round Jasper's neck still irritated and excited him. "The hussy!" he thought. "Smiling—eh? That's how you are amusing yourself. Fooling your father finely, aren't you? You have a taste for that sort of fun—have you? Well, we shall see——" He did not alter his position, but on his pursed-up lips there also appeared a smile of surly and ill-omened amusement, while his eyes returned to the contemplation of his boots.

Freya felt hot with indignation. She sat radiantly fair in the lamplight, her strong, well-shaped hands lying one on top of the other in her lap. . . . "Odious creature," she thought. Her face coloured with sudden anger. "You have scared my maid out of her senses," she said aloud. "What possessed you?"

He was thinking so deeply of her that the sound of her voice, pronouncing these unexpected words, startled him extremely. He jerked up his head and looked so bewildered that Freya insisted impatiently:

"I mean Antonia. You have bruised her arm. What did you do it for?"

"Do you want to quarrel with me?" he asked thickly, with a sort of amazement. He blinked like an owl. He was funny. Freya, like all women, had a keen sense of the ridiculous in outward appearance.

"Well, no; I don't think I do." She could not help herself. She laughed outright, a clear, nervous laugh in which Heemskirk joined suddenly with a harsh "Ha, ha, ha!"

Voices and footsteps were heard in the passage, and Jasper, with old Nelson, came out. Old Nelson looked at his daughter approvingly, for he liked the lieutenant to be kept in good humour. And he also joined sympathetically in the laugh. "Now, lieutenant, we shall have some dinner," he said, rubbing his hands cheerily. Jasper had gone straight to the balustrade. The sky was full of stars, and in the blue velvety night the cove below had a denser blackness, in which the riding-lights of the brig and of the gunboat glimmered redly, like suspended sparks. "Next time this riding-light glimmers down there, I'll be waiting for her on the quarter-deck to come and say 'Here I am,'" Jasper thought; and his heart seemed to grow bigger in his chest, dilated by an oppressive happiness that nearly wrung out a cry from him. There was no wind. Not a leaf below him stirred, and even the sea was but a still uncomplaining shadow. Far away on the unclouded sky the pale lightning, the heat-lightning of the tropics, played tremulously amongst the low stars in short, faint, mysteriously consecutive flashes, like incomprehensible signals from some distant planet.

The dinner passed off quietly. Freya sat facing her father, calm but pale. Heemskirk affected to talk only to old Nelson. Jasper's behaviour was exemplary. He kept his eyes under control, basking in the sense of Freya's nearness, as people bask in the sun without looking up to heaven. And very soon after dinner was over, mindful of his instructions, he declared that it was time for him to go on board his ship.

Heemskirk did not look up. Ensconced in the

rocking-chair, and puffing at a cheroot, he had the air
of meditating surlily over some odious outbreak. So
at least it seemed to Freya. Old Nelson said at once
"I'll stroll down with you." He had begun a professional conversation about the dangers of the New
Guinea coast, and wanted to relate to Jasper some
experience of his own "over there." Jasper was such
a good listener! Freya made as if to accompany them
but her father frowned, shook his head, and nodded
significantly towards the immovable Heemskirk blow-
ing out smoke with half-closed eyes and protruded lips.
The lieutenant must not be left alone. Take offence,
perhaps.

Freya obeyed these signs. "Perhaps it is better for
me to stay," she thought. Women are not generally
prone to review their own conduct, still less to condemn
it. The embarrassing masculine absurdities are in the
main responsible for its ethics. But, looking at Heemskirk, Freya felt regret and even remorse. His thick
bulk in repose suggested the idea of repletion, but as
a matter of fact he had eaten very little. He had
drunk a great deal, however. The fleshy lobes of his
unpleasant big ears with deeply folded rims were
crimson. They quite flamed in the neighbourhood of
the flat, sallow cheeks. For a considerable time he
did not raise his heavy brown eyelids. To be at the
mercy of such a creature was humiliating; and Freya,
who always ended by being frank with herself, thought
regretfully: "If only I had been open with papa from
the first! But then what an impossible life he would
have led me!" Yes. Men were absurd in many ways;
lovably like Jasper, impracticably like her father,
odiously like that grotesquely supine creature in the
chair. Was it possible to talk him over? Perhaps it
was not necessary? "Oh! I can't talk to him," she

thought. And when Heemskirk, still without looking at her, began resolutely to crush his half-smoked cheroot on the coffee-tray, she took alarm, glided towards the piano, opened it in tremendous haste, and struck the keys before she sat down.

In an instant the verandah, the whole carpetless wooden bungalow raised on piles, became filled with an uproarious, confused resonance. But through it all she heard, she felt on the floor the heavy, prowling footsteps of the lieutenant moving to and fro at her back. He was not exactly drunk, but he was sufficiently primed to make the suggestions of his excited imagination seem perfectly feasible and even clever; beautifully, unscrupulously clever. Freya, aware that he had stopped just behind her, went on playing without turning her head. She played with spirit, brilliantly, a fierce piece of music, but when his voice reached her she went cold all over. It was the voice, not the words. The insolent familiarity of tone dismayed her to such an extent that she could not understand at first what he was saying. His utterance was thick, too.

"I suspected. . . . Of course I suspected something of your little goings on. I am not a child. But from suspecting to seeing—seeing, you understand—there's an enormous difference. That sort of thing. . . . Come! One isn't made of stone. And when a man has been worried by a girl as I have been worried by you, Miss Freya—sleeping and waking, then, of course. . . . But I am a man of the world. It must be dull for you here . . . I say, won't you leave off this confounded playing . . . ?"

This last was the only sentence really which she made out. She shook her head negatively, and in desperation put on the loud pedal, but she could not make the sound of the piano cover his raised voice.

"Only, I am surprised that you should. . . . An English trading skipper, a common fellow. Low, cheeky lot, infesting these islands. I would make short work of such trash! While you have here a good friend, a gentleman ready to worship at your feet—your pretty feet—an officer, a man of family. Strange, isn't it? But what of that! You are fit for a prince."

Freya did not turn her head. Her face went stiff with horror and indignation. This adventure was altogether beyond her conception of what was possible. It was not in her character to jump up and run away. It seemed to her, too, that if she did move there was no saying what might happen. Presently her father would be back, and then the other would have to leave off. It was best to ignore—to ignore. She went on playing loudly and correctly, as though she were alone, as if Heemskirk did not exist. That proceeding irritated him.

"Come! You may deceive your father," he bawled angrily, "but I am not to be made a fool of! Stop this infernal noise . . . Freya . . . Hey! You Scandinavian Goddess of Love! Stop! Do you hear? That's what you are—of love. But the heathen gods are only devils in disguise, and that's what you are, too—a deep little devil. Stop it, I say, or I will lift you off that stool!"

Standing behind her, he devoured her with his eyes, from the golden crown of her rigidly motionless head to the heels of her shoes, the line of her shapely shoulders, the curves of her fine figure swaying a little before the keyboard. She had on a light dress; the sleeves stopped short at the elbows in an edging of lace. A satin ribbon encircled her waist. In an access of irresistible, reckless hopefulness he clapped both his hands on that waist—and then the irritating music stopped at last. But,

quick as she was in springing away from the contact
(the round music-stool going over with a crash), Heemskirk's lips, aiming at her neck, landed a hungry, smack-
ing kiss just under her ear. A deep silence reigned for a
time. And then he laughed rather feebly.

He was disconcerted somewhat by her white, still
face, the big light violet eyes resting on him stonily.
She had not uttered a sound. She faced him, steadying
herself on the corner of the piano with one extended
hand. The other went on rubbing with mechanical
persistency the place his lips had touched.

"What's the trouble?" he said, offended. "Startled
you? Look here: don't let us have any of that nonsense. You don't mean to say a kiss frightens you so
much as all that. . . . I know better. . . . I
don't mean to be left out in the cold."

He had been gazing into her face with such strained
intentness that he could no longer see it distinctly.
Everything round him was rather misty. He forgot
the overturned stool, caught his foot against it, and
lurched forward slightly, saying in an ingratiating tone:

"I'm not bad fun, really. You try a few kisses to
begin with——"

He said no more, because his head received a terrific
concussion, accompanied by an explosive sound. Freya
had swung her round, strong arm with such force that
the impact of her open palm on his flat cheek turned
him half round. Uttering a faint, hoarse yell, the
lieutenant clapped both his hands to the left side of
his face, which had taken on suddenly a dusky brick-red
tinge. Freya, very erect, her violet eyes darkened,
her palm still tingling from the blow, a sort of restrained
determined smile showing a tiny gleam of her white
teeth, heard her father's rapid, heavy tread on the
path below the verandah. Her expression lost its

pugnacity and became sincerely concerned. She was sorry for her father. She stooped quickly to pick up the music-stool, as if anxious to obliterate the traces. . . . But that was no good. She had resumed her attitude, one hand resting lightly on the piano, before old Nelson got up to the top of the stairs.

Poor father! How furious he will be—how upset! And afterwards, what tremors, what unhappiness! Why had she not been open with him from the first? His round, innocent stare of amazement cut her to the quick. But he was not looking at her. His stare was directed to Heemskirk, who, with his back to him and with his hands still up to his face, was hissing curses through his teeth, and (she saw him in profile) glaring at her balefully with one black, evil eye.

"What's the matter?" asked old Nelson, very much bewildered.

She did not answer him. She thought of Jasper on the deck of the brig, gazing up at the lighted bungalow, and she felt frightened. It was a mercy that one of them at least was on board out of the way. She only wished he were a hundred miles off. And yet she was not certain that she did. Had Jasper been mysteriously moved that moment to reappear on the verandah she would have thrown her consistency, her firmness, her self-possession, to the winds, and flown into his arms.

"What is it? What is it?" insisted the unsuspecting Nelson, getting quite excited. "Only this minute you were playing a tune, and——"

Freya, unable to speak in her apprehension of what was coming (she was also fascinated by that black, evil, glaring eye), only nodded slightly at the lieutenant, as much as to say: "Just look at him!"

"Why, yes!" exclaimed old Nelson. "I see. What on earth——"

Meantime he had cautiously approached Heemskirk, who, bursting into incoherent imprecations, was stamping with both feet where he stood. The indignity of the blow, the rage of baffled purpose, the ridicule of the exposure, and the impossibility of revenge maddened him to a point when he simply felt he must howl with fury.

"Oh, oh, oh!" he howled, stamping across the verandah as though he meant to drive his foot through the floor at every step.

"Why, is his face hurt?" asked the astounded old Nelson. The truth dawned suddenly upon his innocent mind. "Dear me!" he cried, enlightened. "Get some brandy, quick, Freya. . . . You are subject to it, lieutenant? Fiendish, eh? I know, I know! Used to go crazy all of a sudden myself at the time. . . . And the little bottle of laudanum from the medicine-chest, too, Freya. Look sharp. . . . Don't you see he's got a toothache?"

And, indeed, what other explanation could have presented itself to the guileless old Nelson, beholding this cheek nursed with both hands, these wild glances, these stampings, this distracted swaying of the body? It would have demanded a preternatural acuteness to hit upon the true cause. Freya had not moved. She watched Heemskirk's savagely inquiring, black stare directed stealthily upon herself. "Aha, you would like to be let off!" she said to herself. She looked at him unflinchingly, thinking it out. The temptation of making an end of it all without further trouble was irresistible. She gave an almost imperceptible nod of assent, and glided away.

"Hurry up that brandy!" old Nelson shouted, as she disappeared in the passage.

Heemskirk relieved his deeper feelings by a sudden string of curses in Dutch and English which he sent after her. He raved to his heart's content, flinging to and fro the verandah and kicking chairs out of his way; while Nelson (or Nielsen), whose sympathy was profoundly stirred by these evidences of agonising pain, hovered round his dear (and dreaded) lieutenant, fussing like an old hen.

"Dear me, dear me! Is it so bad? I know well what it is. I used to frighten my poor wife sometimes. Do you get it often like this, lieutenant?"

Heemskirk shouldered him viciously out of his way, with a short, insane laugh. But his staggering host took it in good part; a man beside himself with excruciating toothache is not responsible.

"Go into my room, lieutenant," he suggested urgently. "Throw yourself on my bed. We will get something to ease you in a minute."

He seized the poor sufferer by the arm and forced him gently onwards to the very bed, on which Heemskirk, in a renewed access of rage, flung himself down with such force that he rebounded from the mattress to the height of quite a foot.

"Dear me!" exclaimed the scared Nelson, and incontinently ran off to hurry up the brandy and the laudanum, very angry that so little alacrity was shown in relieving the tortures of his precious guest. In the end he got these things himself.

Half an hour later he stood in the inner passage of the house, surprised by faint, spasmodic sounds of a mysterious nature, between laughter and sobs. He frowned; then went straight towards his daughter's room and knocked at the door.

Freya, her glorious fair hair framing her white face and rippling down a dark-blue dressing-gown, opened it partly.

The light in the room was dim. Antonia, crouching

in a corner, rocked herself backwards and forwards, uttering feeble moans. Old Nelson had not much experience in various kinds of feminine laughter, but he was certain there had been laughter there.

"Very unfeeling, very unfeeling!" he said, with weighty displeasure. "What is there so amusing in a man being in pain? I should have thought a woman —a young girl——"

"He was so funny," murmured Freya, whose eyes glistened strangely in the semi-obscurity of the passage. "And then, you know, I don't like him," she added, in an unsteady voice.

"Funny!" repeated old Nelson, amazed at this evidence of callousness in one so young. "You don't like him! Do you mean to say that, because you don't like him, you—— Why, it's simply cruel! Don't you know it's about the worst sort of pain there is? Dogs have been known to go mad with it."

"He certainly seemed to have gone mad," Freya said with an effort, as if she were struggling with some hidden feeling.

But her father was launched.

"And you know how he is. He notices everything. He is a fellow to take offence for the least little thing —regular Dutchman—and I want to keep friendly with him. It's like this, my girl: if that rajah of ours were to do something silly—and you know he is a sulky, rebellious beggar—and the authorities took into their heads that my influence over him wasn't good, you would find yourself without a roof over your head——"

She cried: "What nonsense, father!" in a not very assured tone, and discovered that he was angry, angry enough to achieve irony; yes, old Nelson (or Nielsen), irony! Just a gleam of it.

"Oh, of course, if you have means of your own—a

mansion, a plantation that I know nothing of——"
But he was not capable of sustained irony. "I tell you
they would bundle me out of here," he whispered
forcibly; "without compensation, of course. I know
these Dutch. And the lieutenant's just the fellow to
start the trouble going. He has the ear of influential
officials. I wouldn't offend him for anything—for
anything—on no consideration whatever. . . . What
did you say?"

It was only an inarticulate exclamation. If she ever
had a half-formed intention of telling him everything she
had given it up now. It was impossible, both out of regard for his dignity and for the peace of his poor mind.

"I don't care for him myself very much," old
Nelson's subdued undertone confessed in a sigh. "He's
easier now," he went on, after a silence. "I've given
him up my bed for the night. I shall sleep on my
verandah, in the hammock. No; I can't say I like him
either, but from that to laugh at a man because he's
driven crazy with pain is a long way. You've surprised
me, Freya. That side of his face is quite flushed."

Her shoulders shook convulsively under his hands,
which he laid on her paternally. His straggly, wiry
moustache brushed her forehead in a good-night kiss.
She closed the door, and went away from it to the
middle of the room before she allowed herself a tired-out
sort of laugh, without buoyancy.

"Flushed! A little flushed!" she repeated to herself.
"I hope so, indeed! A little——"

Her eyelashes were wet. Antonia, in her corner,
moaned and giggled, and it was impossible to tell where
the moans ended and the giggles began.

The mistress and the maid had been somewhat
hysterical, for Freya, on fleeing into her room, had
found Antonia there, and had told her everything.

"I have avenged you, my girl," she exclaimed.

And then they had laughingly cried and cryingly laughed with admonitions—"Ssh, not so loud! Be quiet!" on one part, and interludes of "I am so frightened. . . . He's an evil man," on the other.

Antonia was very much afraid of Heemskirk. She was afraid of him because of his personal appearance: because of his eyes and his eyebrows, and his mouth and his nose and his limbs. Nothing could be more rational. And she thought him an evil man, because, to her eyes, he looked evil. No ground for an opinion could be sounder. In the dimness of the room, with only a nightlight burning at the head of Freya's bed, the camerista crept out of her corner to crouch at the feet of her mistress, supplicating in whispers:

"There's the brig. Captain Allen. Let us run away at once—oh, let us run away! I am so frightened. Let us! Let us!"

"I! Run away!" thought Freya to herself, without looking down at the scared girl. "Never."

Both the resolute mistress under the mosquito-net and the frightened maid lying curled up on a mat at the foot of the bed did not sleep very well that night. The person that did not sleep at all was Lieutenant Heemskirk. He lay on his back staring vindictively in the darkness. Inflaming images and humiliating reflections succeeded each other in his mind, keeping up, augmenting his anger. A pretty tale this to get about! But it must not be allowed to get about. The outrage had to be swallowed in silence. A pretty affair! Fooled, led on, and struck by the girl—and probably fooled by the father, too. But no. Nielsen was but another victim of that shameless hussy, that brazen minx, that sly, laughing, kissing, lying . . .

"No; he did not deceive me on purpose," thought

the tormented lieutenant. "But I should like to pay him off, all the same, for being such an imbecile——"

Well, some day, perhaps. One thing he was firmly resolved on: he had made up his mind to steal early out of the house. He did not think he could face the girl without going out of his mind with fury.

"Fire and perdition! Ten thousand devils! I shall choke here before the morning!" he muttered to himself, lying rigid on his back on old Nelson's bed, his breast heaving for air.

He arose at daylight and started cautiously to open the door. Faint sounds in the passage alarmed him, and remaining concealed he saw Freya coming out. This unexpected sight deprived him of all power to move away from the crack of the door. It was the narrowest crack possible, but commanding the view of the end of the verandah. Freya made for that end hastily to watch the brig passing the point. She wore her dark dressing-gown; her feet were bare, because, having fallen asleep towards the morning, she ran out headlong in her fear of being too late. Heemskirk had never seen her looking like this, with her hair drawn back smoothly to the shape of her head, and hanging in one heavy, fair tress down her back, and with that air of extreme youth, intensity, and eagerness. And at first he was amazed, and then he gnashed his teeth. He could not face her at all. He muttered a curse, and kept still behind the door.

With a low, deep-breathed "Ah!" when she first saw the brig already under way, she reached for Nelson's long glass reposing on brackets high up the wall. The wide sleeve of the dressing-gown slipped back, un-covering her white arm as far as the shoulder. Heemskirk gripping the door-handle, as if to crush it, felt like a man just risen to his feet from a drinking bout.

And Freya knew that he was watching her. She knew. She had seen the door move as she came out of the passage. She was aware of his eyes being on her, with scornful bitterness, with triumphant contempt.

"You are there," she thought, levelling the long glass. "Oh, well, look on, then!"

The green islets appeared like black shadows, the ashen sea was smooth as glass, the clear robe of the colourless dawn, in which even the brig appeared shadowy, had a hem of light in the east. Directly Freya had made out Jasper on deck with his own long glass directed to the bungalow, she laid hers down and raised both her beautiful white arms above her head. In that attitude of supreme cry she stood still, glowing with the consciousness of Jasper's adoration going out to her figure held in the field of his glass away there, and warmed, too, by the feeling of evil passion, the burning, covetous eyes of the other, fastened on her back. In the fervour of her love, in the caprice of her mind, and with that mysterious knowledge of masculine nature women seem to be born to, she thought:

"You are looking on—you will—you must! Then you shall see something."

She brought both her hands to her lips, then flung them out, sending a kiss over the sea, as if she wanted to throw her heart along with it on the deck of the brig. Her face was rosy, her eyes shone. Her repeated, passionate gesture seemed to fling kisses by the hundred again and again and again, while the slowly ascending sun brought the glory of colour to the world, turning the islets green, the sea blue, the brig below her white— dazzlingly white in the spread of her wings—with the red ensign streaming like a tiny flame from the peak. And each time she murmured with a rising inflexion: "Take this—and this—and this——" till suddenly her arms fell. She had seen the ensign dipped in response, and next moment the point below hid the hull of the brig from her view. Then she turned away from the balustrade, and, passing slowly before the door of her father's room with her eyelids lowered, and an enigmatic expression on her face, she disappeared behind the curtain.

But instead of going along the passage, she remained concealed and very still on the other side to watch what would happen. For some time the broad, furnished verandah remained empty. Then the door of old Nelson's room came open suddenly, and Heemskirk staggered out. His hair was rumpled, his eyes bloodshot, his unshaven face looked very dark. He gazed wildly about, saw his cap on a table, snatched it up, and made for the stairs quietly, but with a strange, tottering gait, like the last effort of waning strength.

Shortly after his head had sunk below the level of the floor, Freya came out from behind the curtain, with compressed, scheming lips, and no softness at all in her luminous eyes. He could not be allowed to sneak off scot free. Never—never! She was excited, she tingled all over, she had tasted blood! He must be made to understand that she had been aware of having been watched; he must know that he had been seen slinking off shamefully. But to run to the front rail and shout after him would have been childish, crude—undignified. And to shout—what? What word? What phrase? No; it was impossible. Then how? . . . She frowned, discovered it, dashed at the piano, which had stood open all night, and made the rosewood monster growl savagely in an irritated bass. She struck chords as if firing shots after that straddling, broad figure in ample white trousers and a dark uniform jacket with gold shoulder-straps, and then she pursued him with the same thing she had played the evening before—a modern, fierce piece of love music which had been tried more than once against the thunderstorms of the group. She accentuated its rhythm with triumphant malice, so absorbed in her purpose that she did not notice the presence of her father, who, wearing an old threadbare ulster of a check pattern over his sleeping-suit, had run out from the back verandah to inquire the reason of this untimely performance. He stared at her.

"What on earth? . . . Freya!" . . . His voice was nearly drowned by the piano. "What's become of the lieutenant?" he shouted.

She looked up at him as if her soul were lost in her music, with unseeing eyes.

"Gone."

"Wha-a-t? . . . Where?"

She shook her head slightly, and went on playing louder than before. Old Nelson's innocently anxious gaze starting from the open door of his room, explored the whole place high and low, as if the lieutenant were something small which might have been crawling on the floor or clinging to a wall. But a shrill whistle coming somewhere from below pierced the ample volume of sound rolling out of the piano in great, vibrating waves. The lieutenant was down at the cove, whistling for the boat to come and take him off to his ship. And he seemed to be in a terrific hurry, too, for he whistled again almost directly, waited for a moment, and then sent out a long, interminable shrill call as distressful to hear as though he had shrieked without drawing breath. Freya ceased playing suddenly.

"Going on board," said old Nelson, perturbed by the event. "What could have made him clear out so early? Queer chap. Devilishly touchy, too! I shouldn't wonder if it was your conduct last night that

hurt his feelings. I noticed you, Freya. You as well
as laughed in his face, while he was suffering agonies
from neuralgia. It isn't the way to get yourself liked.
He's offended with you."

Freya's hands now reposed passive on the keys; she
bowed her fair head, feeling a sudden discontent, a nervous
lassitude, as though she had passed through some ex-
hausting crisis. Old Nelson (or Nielsen), looking aggrieved, was revolving matters of policy in his bald head.

"I think it would be right for me to go on board just
to inquire, some time this morning," he declared
fussily. "Why don't they bring me my morning tea?
Do you hear, Freya? You have astonished me, I must
say. I didn't think a young girl could be so unfeeling.
And the lieutenant thinks himself a friend of ours, too!
What? No? Well, he calls himself a friend, and that's
something to a person in my position. Certainly!
Oh, yes, I must go on board."

"Must you?" murmured Freya listlessly; then added
in her thought: "Poor man!"

V

IN RESPECT of the next seven weeks, all that is necessary to say is, first, that old Nelson (or Nielsen) failed
in paying his politic call. The *Neptun* gunboat of H. M.
the King of the Netherlands, commanded by an outraged and infuriated lieutenant, left the cove at an
unexpectedly early hour. When Freya's father came
down to the shore, after seeing his precious crop of
tobacco spread out properly in the sun, she was already
steaming round the point. Old Nelson regretted the
circumstance for many days.

"Now, I don't know in what disposition the man went
away," he lamented to his hard daughter. He was

amazed at her hardness. He was almost frightened by her indifference.

Next, it must be recorded that the same day the gunboat *Neptun*, steering east, passed the brig *Bonito* becalmed in sight of Carimata, with her head to the eastward, too. Her captain, Jasper Allen, giving himself up consciously to a tender, possessive reverie of his Freya, did not get out of his long chair on the poop to look at the *Neptun* which passed so close that the smoke belching out suddenly from her short black funnel rolled between the masts of the *Bonito*, obscuring for a moment the sunlit whiteness of her sails, consecrated to the service of love. Jasper did not even turn his head for a glance. But Heemskirk, on the bridge, had gazed long and earnestly at the brig from the distance, gripping hard the brass rail in front of him, till, the two ships closing, he lost all confidence in himself, and retreating to the chartroom, pulled the door to with a crash. There, his brows knitted, his mouth drawn on one side in sardonic meditation, he sat through many still hours—a sort of Prometheus in the bonds of unholy desire, having his very vitals torn by the beak and claws of humiliated passion.

That species of fowl is not to be shooed off as easily as a chicken. Fooled, cheated, deceived, led on, outraged, mocked at—beak and claws! A sinister bird! The lieutenant had no mind to become the talk of the Archipelago, as the naval officer who had had his face slapped by a girl. Was it possible that she really loved that rascally trader? He tried not to think, but worse than thoughts, definite impressions beset him in his retreat. He saw her—a vision plain, close to, detailed, plastic, coloured, lighted up—he saw her hanging round the neck of that fellow. And he shut his eyes, only to discover that this was no remedy.

Then a piano began to play near by, very plainly; and he put his fingers to his ears with no better effect. It was not to be borne—not in solitude. He bolted out of the chartroom, and talked of indifferent things somewhat wildly with the officer of the watch on the bridge, to the mocking accompaniment of a ghostly piano.

The last thing to be recorded is that Lieutenant Heemskirk instead of pursuing his course towards Ternate, where he was expected, went out of his way to call at Makassar, where no one was looking for his arrival. Once there, he gave certain explanations and laid a certain proposal before the governor, or some other authority, and obtained permission to do what he thought fit in these matters. Thereupon the *Neptun*, giving up Ternate altogether, steamed north in view of the mountainous coast of Celebes, and then crossing the broad straits took up her station on the low coast of virgin forests, inviolate and mute, in waters phosphorescent at night, deep blue in daytime with gleaming green patches over the submerged reefs. For days the *Neptun* could be seen moving smoothly up and down the sombre face of the shore, or hanging about with a watchful air near the silvery breaks of broad estuaries, under the great luminous sky never softened, never veiled, and flooding the earth with the everlasting sunshine of the tropics—that sunshine which, in its unbroken splendour, oppresses the soul with an inexpressible melancholy more intimate, more penetrating, more profound than the grey sadness of the northern mists.

．　　　．　　　．　　　．　　　．　　　．　　　．

The trading brig *Bonito* appeared gliding round a sombre forest-clad point of land on the silvery estuary of a great river. The breath of air that gave her motion would not have fluttered the flame of a torch. She stole out into the open from behind a veil of un-stirring leaves, mysteriously silent, ghostly white, and solemnly stealthy in her imperceptible progress; and Jasper, his elbow in the main rigging, and his head leaning against his hand, thought of Freya. Everything in the world reminded him of her. The beauty of the loved woman exists in the beauties of Nature. The swelling outlines of the hills, the curves of a coast, the free sinuosities of a river are less suave than the harmonious lines of her body, and when she moves, gliding lightly, the grace of her progress suggests the power of occult forces which rule the fascinating aspects of the visible world.

Dependent on things as all men are, Jasper loved his vessel—the house of his dreams. He lent to her something of Freya's soul. Her deck was the foothold of their love. The possession of his brig appeased his passion in a soothing certitude of happiness already conquered.

The full moon was some way up, perfect and serene, floating in air as calm and limpid as the glance of Freya's eyes. There was not a sound in the brig.

"Here she will stand, by my side, on evenings like this," he thought, with rapture.

And it was at that moment, in this peace, in this serenity, under the full, benign gaze of the moon propitious to lovers, on a sea without a wrinkle, under a sky without a cloud, as if all Nature had assumed its most clement mood in a spirit of mockery, that the gunboat *Neptun*, detaching herself from the dark coast under which she had been lying invisible, steamed out to intercept the trading brig *Bonito* standing out to sea.

Directly the gunboat had been made out emerging

from her ambush, Schultz, of the fascinating voice, had given signs of strange agitation. All that day, ever since leaving the Malay town up the river, he had shown a haggard face, going about his duties like a man with something weighing on his mind. Jasper had noticed it, but the mate, turning away, as though he had not liked being looked at, had muttered shamefacedly of a headache and a touch of fever. He must have had it very badly when, dodging behind his captain, he wondered aloud: "What can that fellow want with us?" . . . A naked man standing in a freezing blast and trying not to shiver could not have spoken with a more harshly uncertain intonation. But it might have been fever—a cold fit.

"He wants to make himself disagreeable, simply," said Jasper, with perfect good humour. "He has tried it on me before. However, we shall soon see."

And, indeed, before long the two vessels lay abreast within easy hail. The brig, with her fine lines and her white sails, looked vaporous and sylph-like in the moonlight. The gunboat, short, squat, with her stumpy dark spars naked like dead trees, raised against the luminous sky of that resplendent night, threw a heavy shadow on the lane of water between the two ships.

Freya haunted them both like an ubiquitous spirit, and as if she were the only woman in the world. Jasper remembered her earnest recommendation to be guarded and cautious in all his acts and words while he was away from her. In this quite unforeseen encounter he felt on his ear the very breath of these hurried admonitions customary to the last moment of their partings, heard the half-jesting final whisper of the "Mind, kid, I'd never forgive you!" with a quick pressure on his arm, which he answered by a quiet, confident smile. Heemskirk was haunted in another fashion. There were no whispers in it; it was more like visions. He saw that girl hanging round the neck of a low vagabond—*that* vagabond, the vagabond who had just answered his hail. He saw her stealing barefooted across a verandah with great, clear, wide-open, eager eyes to look at a brig—*that* brig. If she had shrieked, scolded, called names! . . . But she had simply triumphed over him. That was all. Led on (he firmly believed it), fooled, deceived, outraged, struck, mocked at. . . . Beak and claws! The two men, so differently haunted by Freya of the Seven Isles, were not equally matched.

In the intense stillness, as of sleep, which had fallen upon the two vessels, in a world that itself seemed but a delicate dream, a boat pulled by Javanese sailors crossing the dark lane of water came alongside the brig. The white warrant officer in her, perhaps the gunner, climbed aboard. He was a short man, with a rotund stomach and a wheezy voice. His immovable fat face looked lifeless in the moonlight, and he walked with his thick arms hanging away from his body as though he had been stuffed. His cunning little eyes glittered like bits of mica. He conveyed to Jasper, in broken English, a request to come on board the *Neptun*.

Jasper had not expected anything so unusual. But after a short reflection he decided to show neither annoyance, nor even surprise. The river from which he had come had been politically disturbed for a couple of years, and he was aware that his visits there were looked upon with some suspicion. But he did not mind much the displeasure of the authorities, so terrifying to old Nelson. He prepared to leave the brig, and Schultz followed him to the rail as if to say something, but in the end stood by in silence. Jasper getting over the side, noticed his ghastly face. The eyes of the man who had found salvation in the brig from the effects of his peculiar psychology looked at him with a dumb, beseeching expression.

"What's the matter?" Jasper asked.

"I wonder how this will end?" said he of the beautiful voice, which had even fascinated the steady Freya herself. But where was its charming timbre now? These words had sounded like a raven's croak.

"You are ill," said Jasper positively.

"I wish I were dead!" was the startling statement uttered by Schultz talking to himself in the extremity of some mysterious trouble. Jasper gave him a keen glance, but this was not the time to investigate the morbid outbreak of a feverish man. He did not look as though he were actually delirious, and that for the moment must suffice. Schultz made a dart forward.

"That fellow means harm!" he said desperately. "He means harm to you, Captain Allen. I feel it, and I——"

He choked with inexplicable emotion.

"All right, Schultz. I won't give him an opening." Jasper cut him short and swung himself into the boat.

On board the *Neptun* Heemskirk, standing straddle-legs in the flood of moonlight, his inky shadow falling right across the quarter-deck, made no sign at his approach, but secretly he felt something like the heave of the sea in his chest at the sight of that man. Jasper waited before him in silence.

Brought face to face in direct personal contact, they fell at once into the manner of their casual meetings in old Nelson's bungalow. They ignored each other's existence—Heemskirk moodily; Jasper, with a perfectly colourless quietness.

"What's going on in that river you've just come out of?" asked the lieutenant straight away.

"I know nothing of the troubles, if you mean that," Jasper answered. "I've landed there half a cargo of rice, for which I got nothing in exchange, and went away. There's no trade there now, but they would have been starving in another week if I hadn't turned up."

"Meddling! English meddling! And suppose the rascals don't deserve anything better than to starve, eh?"

"There are women and children there, you know," observed Jasper, in his even tone.

"Oh, yes! When an Englishman talks of women and children, you may be sure there's something fishy about the business. Your doings will have to be investigated."

They spoke in turn, as though they had been disembodied spirits—mere voices in empty air; for they looked at each other as if there had been nothing there, or, at most, with as much recognition as one gives to an inanimate object, and no more. But now a silence fell. Heemskirk had thought, all at once: "She will tell him all about it. She will tell him while she hangs round his neck laughing." And the sudden desire to annihilate Jasper on the spot almost deprived him of his senses by its vehemence. He lost the power of speech, of vision. For a moment he absolutely couldn't see Jasper. But he heard him inquiring, as of the world at large:

"Am I, then, to conclude that the brig is detained?"

Heemskirk made a recovery in a flush of malignant satisfaction.

"She is. I am going to take her to Makassar in tow."

"The courts will have to decide on the legality of this," said Jasper, aware that the matter was becoming serious, but with assumed indifference.

"Oh, yes, the courts! Certainly. And as to you, I shall keep you on board here."

Jasper's dismay at being parted from his ship was betrayed by a stony immobility. It lasted but an instant. Then he turned away and hailed the brig. Mr. Schultz answered:

"Yes, sir."

"Get ready to receive a tow-rope from the gunboat! We are going to be taken to Makassar."

"Good God! What's that for, sir?" came an anxious cry faintly.

"Kindness, I suppose," Jasper, ironical, shouted with great deliberation. "We might have been—becalmed in here—for days. And hospitality. I am invited to stay—on board here."

The answer to this information was a loud ejaculation of distress. Jasper thought anxiously: "Why, the fellow's nerve's gone to pieces;" and with an awkward uneasiness of a new sort, looked intently at the brig. The thought that he was parted from her—for the first time since they came together—shook the apparently careless fortitude of his character to its very foundations, which were deep. All that time neither Heemskirk nor even his inky shadow had stirred in the least.

"I am going to send a boat's crew and an officer on board your vessel," he announced to no one in particular. Jasper, tearing himself away from the absorbed contemplation of the brig, turned round, and, without passion, almost without expression in his voice, entered his protest against the whole of the proceedings. What he was thinking of was the delay. He counted the days. Makassar was actually on his way; and to be towed there really saved time. On the other hand, there would be some vexing formalities to go through.

But the thing was too absurd. "The beetle's gone mad," he thought. "I'll be released at once. And if not, Mesman must enter into a bond for me." Mesman was a Dutch merchant with whom Jasper had had many dealings, a considerable person in Makassar.

"You protest? H'm!" Heemskirk muttered, and for a little longer remained motionless, his legs planted well apart, and his head lowered as though he were studying his own comical deeply split shadow. Then he made a sign to the rotund gunner, who had kept at hand, motionless, like a vilely stuffed specimen of a fat man, with a lifeless face and glittering little eyes. The fellow approached, and stood at attention.

"You will board the brig with a boat's crew!"

"Ya, mynherr!"

"You will have one of your men to steer her all the time," went on Heemskirk, giving his orders in English, apparently for Jasper's edification. "You hear?"

"Ya, mynherr."

"You will remain on deck and in charge all the time."

"Ya, mynherr."

Jasper felt as if, together with the command of the brig, his very heart were being taken out of his breast. Heemskirk asked, with a change of tone:

"What weapons have you on board?"

At one time all the ships trading in the China Seas had a licence to carry a certain quantity of firearms for purposes of defence. Jasper answered:

"Eighteen rifles with their bayonets, which were on board when I bought her, four years ago. They have been declared."

"Where are they kept?"

"Fore-cabin. Mate has the key."

"You will take possession of them," said Heemskirk to the gunner.

"Ya, mynherr."

"What is this for? What do you mean to imply?" cried out Jasper; then bit his lip. "It's monstrous!" he muttered.

Heemskirk raised for a moment a heavy, as if suffering, glance.

"You may go," he said to his gunner. The fat man saluted, and departed.

During the next thirty hours the steady towing was interrupted once. At a signal from the brig, made by waving a flag on the forecastle, the gunboat was stopped. The badly stuffed specimen of a warrant-officer, getting into his boat, arrived on board the *Neptun* and hurried straight into his commander's cabin, his excitement at something he had to communicate being betrayed by the blinking of his small eyes. These two were closeted together for some time, while Jasper at the taffrail tried to make out if anything out of the common had occurred on board the brig. But nothing seemed to be amiss on board. However, he kept a look-out for the gunner; and, though he had avoided speaking to anybody since he had finished with Heemskirk, he stopped that man when he came out on deck again to ask how his mate was.

"He was feeling not very well when I left," he explained.

The fat warrant-officer, holding himself as though the effort of carrying his big stomach in front of him demanded a rigid carriage, understood with difficulty. Not a single one of his features showed the slightest animation, but his little eyes blinked rapidly at last.

"Oh, ya! The mate. Ya, ya! He is very well. But, mein Gott, he is one very funny man!"

Jasper could get no explanation of that remark, because the Dutchman got into the boat hurriedly, and went back on board the brig. But he consoled himself with the thought that very soon all this unpleasant and rather absurd experience would be over. The roadstead of Makassar was in sight already. Heemskirk passed by him going on the bridge. For the first time the lieutenant looked at Jasper with marked intention; and the strange roll of his eyes was so funny—it had been long agreed by Jasper and Freya that the lieutenant was funny—so ecstatically gratified, as though he were rolling a tasty morsel on his tongue, that Jasper could not help a broad smile. And then he turned to his brig again.

To see her, his cherished possession, animated by something of his Freya's soul, the only foothold of twc lives on the wide earth, the security of his passion, the companion of adventure, the power to snatch the calm, adorable Freya to his breast, and carry her off to the end of the world; to see this beautiful thing embodying worthily his pride and his love, to see her captive at the end of a tow-rope was not indeed a pleasant experience. It had something nightmarish in it, as, for instance, the dream of a wild sea-bird loaded with chains.

Yet what else could he want to look at? Her beauty would sometimes come to his heart with the force of a spell, so that he would forget where he was. And, besides, that sense of superiority which the certitude of being loved gives to a young man, that illusion of being set above the Fates by a tender look in a woman's eyes, helped him, the first shock over, to go through these experiences with an amused self-confidence. For what evil could touch the elect of Freya?

It was now afternoon, the sun being behind the two vessels as they headed for the harbour. "The beetle's little joke will soon be over," thought Jasper, without

any great animosity. As a seaman well acquainted
with that part of the world, a casual glance was enough
to tell him what was being done. "Hallo," he thought,
"he is going through Spermonde Passage. We shall
be rounding Tamissa reef presently." And again he
returned to the contemplation of his brig, that main-
stay of his material and emotional existence which
would be soon in his hands again. On a sea, calm
as a millpond, a heavy smooth ripple undulated and
streamed away from her bows, for the powerful *Neptun*
was towing at great speed, as if for a wager. The
Dutch gunner appeared on the forecastle of the *Bonito*,
and with him a couple of men. They stood looking at
the coast, and Jasper lost himself in a loverlike trance.

The deep-toned blast of the gunboat's steam-whistle
made him shudder by its unexpectedness. Slowly he
looked about. Swift as lightning he leaped from where
he stood, bounding forward along the deck.

"You will be on Tamissa reef!" he yelled.

High up on the bridge Heemskirk looked back over
his shoulder heavily; two seamen were spinning the
wheel round, and the *Neptun* was already swinging
rapidly away from the edge of the pale water over the
danger. Ha! Just in time. Jasper turned about
instantly to watch his brig; and, even before he realised
that—in obedience, it appears, to Heemskirk's orders
given beforehand to the gunner—the tow-rope had been
let go at the blast of the whistle, before he had time to
cry out or to move a limb, he saw her cast adrift and
shooting across the gunboat's stern with the impetus of
her speed. He followed her fine, gliding form with eyes
growing big with incredulity, wild with horror. The
cries on board of her came to him only as a dreadful and
confused murmur through the loud thumping of blood
in his ears, while she held on. She ran upright in a

terrible display of her gift of speed, with an incom-
parable air of life and grace. She ran on till the smooth
level of water in front of her bows seemed to sink down
suddenly as if sucked away; and, with a strange, violent
tremor of her mastheads she stopped, inclined her lofty
spars a little, and lay still. She lay still on the reef,
while the *Neptun*, fetching a wide circle, continued at
full speed up Spermonde Passage, heading for the town.
She lay still, perfectly still, with something ill-omened
and unnatural in her attitude. In an instant the subtle
melancholy of things touched by decay had fallen on
her in the sunshine; she was but a speck in the brilliant
emptiness of space, already lonely, already desolate.

"Hold him!" yelled a voice from the bridge.

Jasper had started to run to his brig with a headlong
impulse, as a man dashes forward to pull away with
his hands a living, breathing, loved creature from the
brink of destruction. "Hold him! Stick to him!"
vociferated the lieutenant at the top of the bridge-
ladder, while Jasper struggled madly without a word,
only his head emerging from the heaving crowd of the
Neptun's seamen, who had flung themselves upon him
obediently. "Hold—— I would not have that fellow
drown himself for anything now!"

Jasper ceased struggling.

One by one they let go of him; they fell back gradually
farther and farther, in attentive silence, leaving him
standing unsupported in a widened, clear space, as if to
give him plenty of room to fall after the struggle. He
did not even sway perceptibly. Half an hour later,
when the *Neptun* anchored in front of the town, he had
not stirred yet, had moved neither head nor limb as
much as a hair's breadth. Directly the rumble of the
gunboat's cable had ceased, Heemskirk came down
heavily from the bridge.

"Call a sampan," he said, in a gloomy tone, as he passed the sentry at the gangway, and then moved on slowly towards the spot where Jasper, the object of many awed glances, stood looking at the deck, as if lost in a brown study. Heemskirk came up close, and stared at him thoughtfully, with his fingers over his lips. Here he was, the favoured vagabond, the only man to whom that infernal girl was likely to tell the story. But he would not find it funny. The story how Lieutenant Heemskirk—— No, he would not laugh at it. He looked as though he would never laugh at anything in his life.

Suddenly Jasper looked up. His eyes, without any other expression but bewilderment, met those of Heemskirk, observant and sombre.

"Gone on the reef!" he said, in a low, astounded tone. "On—the—reef!" he repeated still lower and as if attending inwardly to the birth of some awful and amazing sensation.

"On the very top of high-water, spring tides," Heemskirk struck in, with a vindictive, exulting violence which flashed and expired. He paused, as if weary, fixing upon Jasper his arrogant eyes, over which secret disenchantment, the unavoidable shadow of all passion, seemed to pass like a saddening cloud. "On the very top," he repeated, rousing himself in fierce reaction to snatch his laced cap off his head with a horizontal, derisive flourish towards the gangway. "And now you may go ashore to the courts, you damned Englishman!" he said.

VI

THE affair of the brig *Bonito* was bound to cause a sensation in Makassar, the prettiest, and perhaps the cleanest-looking of all the towns in the Islands; which however knows few occasions for excitement. The "front," with its special population, was soon aware that something had happened. A steamer towing a sailing vessel had been observed far out to sea for some time, and when the steamer came in alone, leaving the other outside, attention was aroused. Why was that? Her masts only could be seen—with furled sails— remaining in the same place to the southward. And soon the rumour ran all along the crowded seashore street that there was a ship on Tamissa reef. That crowd interpreted the appearance correctly. Its cause was beyond their penetration, for who could associate a girl nine hundred miles away with the stranding of a ship on Tamissa reef, or look for the remote filiation of that event in the psychology of at least three people, even if one of them, Lieutenant Heemskirk, was at that very moment passing amongst them on his way to make his verbal report?

No; the minds on the "front" were not competent for that sort of investigation, but many hands there —brown hands, yellow hands, white hands—were raised to shade the eyes gazing out to sea. The rumour spread quickly. Chinese shopkeepers came to their doors, more than one white merchant, even, rose from his desk to go to the window. After all, a ship on Tamissa was not an everyday occurrence. And presently the rumour took a more definite shape. An English trader—detained on suspicion at sea by the *Neptun*—Heemskirk was towing him in to test a case, and by some strange accident——

Later on the name came out. "The *Bonito*—what! Impossible! Yes—yes, the *Bonito*. Look! You can see from here; only two masts. It's a brig. Didn't think that man would ever let himself be caught.

Heemskirk's pretty smart, too. They say she's fitted out in her cabin like a gentleman's yacht. That Allen is a sort of gentleman too. An extravagant beggar."

A young man entered smartly Messrs. Mesman Brothers' office on the "front," bubbling with some further information.

"Oh, yes; that's the *Bonito* for certain! But you don't know the story I've heard just now. The fellow must have been feeding that river with firearms for the last year or two. Well, it seems he has grown so reckless from long impunity that he has actually dared to sell the very ship's rifles this time. It's a fact. The rifles are not on board. What impudence! Only, he didn't know that there was one of our warships on the coast. But those Englishmen are so impudent that perhaps he thought that nothing would be done to him for it. Our courts do let off these fellows too often, on some miserable excuse or other. But, at any rate, there's an end of the famous *Bonito*. I have just heard in the harbour-office that she must have gone on at the very top of high-water; and she is in ballast, too. No human power, they think, can move her from where she is. I only hope it is so. It would be fine to have the notorious *Bonito* stuck up there as a warning to others."

Mr. J. Mesman, a colonial-born Dutchman, a kind, paternal old fellow, with a clean-shaven, quiet, handsome face, and a head of fine iron-grey hair curling a little on his collar, did not say a word in defence of Jasper and the *Bonito*. He rose from his arm-chair suddenly. His face was visibly troubled. It had so happened that once, from a business talk of ways and means, island trade, money matters, and so on, Jasper had been led to open himself to him on the subject of Freya; and the excellent man, who had known old

Nelson years before and even remembered something of Freya, was much astonished and amused by the unfolding of the tale.

"Well, well, well! Nelson! Yes; of course. A very honest sort of man. And a little child with very fair hair. Oh, yes! I have a distinct recollection. And so she has grown into such a fine girl, so very determined, so very——" And he laughed almost boisterously. "Mind, when you have happily eloped with your future wife, Captain Allen, you must come along this way, and we shall welcome her here. A little fair-headed child! I remember. I remember."

It was that knowledge which had brought trouble to his face at the first news of the wreck. He took up his hat.

"Where are you going, Mr. Mesman?"

"I am going to look for Allen. I think he must be ashore. Does anybody know?"

No one of those present knew. And Mr. Mesman went out on the "front" to make inquiries.

The other part of the town, the part near the church and the fort, got its information in another way. The first thing disclosed to it was Jasper himself walking rapidly, as though he were pursued. And, as a matter of fact, a Chinaman, obviously a sampan man, was following him at the same headlong pace. Suddenly, while passing Orange House, Jasper swerved and went in, or, rather, rushed in, startling Gomez, the hotel clerk, very much. But a Chinaman beginning to make an unseemly noise at the door claimed the immediate attention of Gomez. His grievance was that the white man whom he had brought on shore from the gunboat had not paid him his boat-fare. He had pursued him so far, asking for it all the way. But the white man had taken no notice whatever of his just claim. Gomez satisfied the coolie with a few coppers, and then went to look for Jasper, whom he knew very well. He found him standing stiffly by a little round table. At the other end of the verandah a few men sitting there had stopped talking, and were looking at him in silence. Two billiard-players, with cues in their hands, had come to the door of the billiard-room and stared, too.

On Gomez coming up to him, Jasper raised one hand to point at his own throat. Gomez noted the somewhat soiled state of his white clothes, then took one look at his face, and fled away to order the drink for which Jasper seemed to be asking.

Where he wanted to go—for what purpose—where he, perhaps, only imagined himself to be going, when a sudden impulse or the sight of a familiar place had made him turn into Orange House—it is impossible to say. He was steadying himself lightly with the tips of his fingers on the little table. There were on that verandah two men whom he knew well personally, but his gaze roaming incessantly as though he were looking for a way of escape, passed and repassed over them without a sign of recognition. They, on their side, looking at him, doubted the evidence of their own eyes. It was not that his face was distorted. On the contrary, it was still, it was set. But its expression, somehow, was unrecognisable. Can that be him? they wondered with awe.

In his head there was a wild chaos of clear thoughts. Perfectly clear. It was this clearness which was so terrible in conjunction with the utter inability to lay hold of any single one of them all. He was saying to himself, or to them: "Steady, steady." A China boy appeared before him with a glass on a tray. He poured the drink down his throat, and rushed out. His disappearance removed the spell of wonder from the beholders. One of the men jumped up and moved quickly to that side of the verandah from which almost the whole of the roadstead could be seen. At the very moment when Jasper, issuing from the door of the Orange House, was passing under him in the street below, he cried to the others excitedly:

"That was Allen right enough! But where is his brig?"

Jasper heard these words with extraordinary loudness. The heavens rang with them, as if calling him to account; for those were the very words Freya would have to use. It was an annihilating question; it struck his consciousness like a thunderbolt and brought a sudden night upon the chaos of his thoughts even as he walked. He did not check his pace. He went on in the darkness for another three strides, and then fell.

The good Mesman had to push on as far as the hospital before he found him. The doctor there talked of a slight heatstroke. Nothing very much. Out in three days. . . . It must be admitted that the doctor was right. In three days, Jasper Allen came out of the hospital and became visible to the town—very visible indeed—and remained so for quite a long time; long enough to become almost one of the sights of the place; long enough to become disregarded at last; long enough for the tale of his haunting visibility to be remembered in the islands to this day.

The talk on the "front" and Jasper's appearance in the Orange House stand at the beginning of the famous *Bonito* case, and give a view of its two aspects—the practical and the psychological. The case for the courts and the case for compassion; that last terribly evident and yet obscure.

It has, you must understand, remained obscure

even for that friend of mine who wrote me the letter mentioned in the very first lines of this narrative. He was one of those in Mr. Mesman's office, and accompanied that gentleman in his search for Jasper. His letter described to me the two aspects and some of the episodes of the case. Heemskirk's attitude was that of deep thankfulness for not having lost his own ship, and that was all. Haze over the land was his explanation of having got so close to Tamissa reef. He saved his ship, and for the rest he did not care. As to the fat gunner, he deposed simply that he thought at the time that he was acting for the best by letting go the tow-rope, but admitted that he was greatly confused by the suddenness of the emergency.

As a matter of fact, he had acted on very precise instructions from Heemskirk, to whom through several years' service together in the East he had become a sort of devoted henchman. What was most amazing in the detention of the *Bonito* was his story how, proceeding to take possession of the firearms as ordered, he discovered that there were no firearms on board. All he found in the fore-cabin was an empty rack for the proper number of eighteen rifles, but of the rifles themselves never a single one anywhere in the ship. The mate of the brig, who looked rather ill and behaved excitedly, as though he were perhaps a lunatic, wanted him to believe that Captain Allen knew nothing of this; that it was he, the mate, who had recently sold these rifles in the dead of night to a certain person up the river. In proof of this story he produced a bag of silver dollars and pressed it on his, the gunner's, acceptance. Then, suddenly flinging it down on the deck, he beat his own head with both his fists and started heaping shocking curses upon his own soul for an ungrateful wretch not fit to live.

All this the gunner reported at once to his commanding officer.

What Heemskirk intended by taking upon himself to detain the *Bonito* it is difficult to say, except that he meant to bring some trouble into the life of the man favoured by Freya. He had been looking at Jasper with a desire to strike that man of kisses and embraces to the earth. The question was: How could he do it without giving himself away? But the report of the gunner created a serious case enough. Yet Allen had friends—and who could tell whether he wouldn't somehow succeed in wriggling out of it? The idea of simply towing the brig so much compromised on to the reef came to him while he was listening to the fat gunner in his cabin. There was but little risk of being disapproved now. And it should be made to appear an accident.

Going out on deck he had gloated upon his unconscious victim with such a sinister roll of his eyes, such a queerly pursed mouth, that Jasper could not help smiling. And the lieutenant had gone on the bridge, saying to himself:

"You wait! I shall spoil the taste of those sweet kisses for you. When you hear of Lieutenant Heemskirk in the future that name won't bring a smile on your lips, I swear. You are delivered into my hands."

And this possibility had come about without any planning, one could almost say naturally, as if events had mysteriously shaped themselves to fit the purposes of a dark passion. The most astute scheming could not have served Heemskirk better. It was given to him to taste a transcendental, an incredible perfection of vengeance; to strike a deadly blow into that hated person's heart, and to watch him afterwards walking about with the dagger in his breast.

For that is what the state of Jasper amounted to.

He moved, acted, weary-eyed, keen-faced, lank and restless, with brusque movements and fierce gestures; he talked incessantly in a frenzied and fatigued voice, but within himself he knew that nothing would ever give him back the brig, just as nothing can heal a pierced heart. His soul, kept quiet in the stress of love by the unflinching Freya's influence, was like a still but overwound string. The shock had started it vibrating, and the string had snapped. He had waited for two years in a perfectly intoxicated confidence for a day that now would never come to a man disarmed for life by the loss of the brig, and, it seemed to him, made unfit for love to which he had no foothold to offer.

Day after day he would traverse the length of the town, follow the coast, and, reaching the point of land opposite that part of the reef on which his brig lay stranded, look steadily across the water at her beloved form, once the home of an exulting hope, and now, in her inclined, desolated immobility, towering above the lonely sea-horizon, a symbol of despair.

The crew had left her in due course in her own boats which directly they reached the town were sequestrated by the harbour authorities. The vessel, too, was sequestrated pending proceedings; but these same authorities did not take the trouble to set a guard on board. For, indeed, what could move her from there? Nothing, unless a miracle; nothing, unless Jasper's eyes, fastened on her tensely for hours together, as though he hoped by the mere power of vision to draw her to his breast.

All this story, read in my friend's very chatty letter, dismayed me not a little. But it was really appalling to read his relation of how Schultz, the mate, went about everywhere affirming with desperate pertinacity that it was he alone who had sold the rifles. "I stole them," he protested. Of course, no one would believe him. My friend himself did not believe him, though he, of course, admired this self-sacrifice. But a good many people thought it was going too far to make oneself out a thief for the sake of a friend. Only, it was such an obvious lie, too, that it did not matter, perhaps.

I, who, in view of Schultz's psychology, knew how true that must be, admit that I was appalled. So this was how a perfidious destiny took advantage of a generous impulse! And I felt as though I were an accomplice in this perfidy, since I did to a certain extent encourage Jasper. Yet I had warned him as well.

"The man seemed to have gone crazy on this point," wrote my friend. "He went to Mesman with his story. He says that some rascally white man living amongst the natives up that river made him drunk with some gin one evening, and then jeered at him for never having any money. Then he, protesting to us that he was an honest man and must be believed, described himself as being a thief whenever he took a drop too much, and told us that he went on board and passed the rifles one by one without the slightest compunction to a canoe which came alongside that night, receiving ten dollars apiece for them.

"Next day he was ill with shame and grief, but had not the courage to confess his lapse to his benefactor. When the gunboat stopped the brig he felt ready to die with the apprehension of the consequences, and would have died happily, if he could have been able to bring the rifles back by the sacrifice of his life. He said nothing to Jasper, hoping that the brig would be released presently. When it turned out otherwise and his captain was detained on board the gunboat, he was ready to commit suicide from despair; only he thought it his duty to live in order to let the truth be known. 'I am an honest man! I am an honest man!' he repeated, in a voice that brought tears to our eyes. 'You must believe me when I tell you that I am a thief—a vile, low, cunning, sneaking thief as soon as I've had a glass or two. Take me somewhere where I may tell the truth on oath.'

"When we had at last convinced him that his story could be of no use to Jasper—for what Dutch court, having once got hold of an English trader, would accept such an explanation; and, indeed, how, when, where could one hope to find proofs of such a tale?—he made as if to tear his hair in handfuls, but, calming down, said: 'Good-bye, then, gentlemen,' and went out of the room so crushed that he seemed hardly able to put one foot before the other. That very night he committed suicide by cutting his throat in the house of a half-caste with whom he had been lodging since he came ashore from the wreck."

That throat, I thought with a shudder, which could produce the tender, persuasive, manly, but fascinating voice which had aroused Jasper's ready compassion and had secured Freya's sympathy! Who could ever have supposed such an end in store for the impossible, gentle Schultz, with his idiosyncrasy of naïve pilfering, so absurdly straightforward that, even in the people who had suffered from it, it aroused nothing more than a sort of amused exasperation? He was really impossible. His lot evidently should have been a half-starved, mysterious, but by no means tragic existence as a mild-eyed, inoffensive beachcomber on the fringe of native life. There are occasions when the irony of fate, which some people profess to discover in the working out of our lives, wears the aspect of crude and savage jesting.

I shook my head over the manes of Schultz, and went

on with my friend's letter. It told me how the brig on the reef, looted by the natives from the coast villages, acquired gradually the lamentable aspect, the grey ghostliness of a wreck; while Jasper, fading daily into a mere shadow of a man, strode brusquely all along the "front" with horribly lively eyes and a faint, fixed smile on his lips, to spend the day on a lonely spit of sand looking eagerly at her, as though he had expected some shape on board to rise up and make some sort of sign to him over the decaying bulwarks. The Mesmans were taking care of him as far as it was possible. The *Bonito* case had been referred to Batavia, where no doubt it would fade away in a fog of official papers. . . . It was heartrending to read all this. That active and zealous officer, Lieutenant Heemskirk, his air of sullen, darkly pained self-importance not lightened by the approval of his action conveyed to him unofficially, had gone on to take up his station in the Moluccas. . . .

Then, at the end of the bulky, kindly meant epistle, dealing with the island news of half a year at least, my friend wrote: "A couple of months ago old Nelson turned up here, arriving by the mail-boat from Java. Came to see Mesman, it seems. A rather mysterious visit, and extraordinarily short, after coming all that way. He stayed just four days at the Orange House with apparently nothing in particular to do, and then caught the south-going steamer for the Straits. I remember people saying at one time that Allen was rather sweet on old Nelson's daughter, the girl that was brought up by Mrs. Harley and then went to live with him at the Seven Isles group. Surely you remember old Nelson——"

Remember old Nelson! Rather!

The letter went on to inform me further that old

Nelson, at least, remembered me, since some time after his flying visit to Makassar he had written to the Mesmans asking for my address in London.

That old Nelson (or Nielsen), the note of whose personality was a profound, echoless irresponsiveness to everything around him, should wish to write, or find anything to write about to anybody, was in itself a cause for no small wonder. And to me, of all people! I waited with uneasy impatience for whatever disclosure could come from that naturally benighted intelligence, but my impatience had time to wear out before my eyes beheld old Nelson's trembling, painfully formed hand-writing, senile and childish at the same time, on an envelope bearing a penny stamp and the postal mark of the Notting Hill office. I delayed opening it in order to pay the tribute of astonishment due to the event by flinging my hands above my head. So he had come home to England, to be definitely Nelson; or else was on his way home to Denmark, where he would revert for ever to his original Nielsen! But old Nelson (or Nielsen) out of the tropics seemed unthinkable. And yet he was there, asking me to call.

His address was at a boarding-house in one of those Bayswater squares, once of leisure, which nowadays are reduced to earning their living. Somebody had recommended him there. I started to call on him on one of those January days in London, one of those wintry days composed of the four devilish elements, cold, wet, mud, and grime, combined with a particular stickiness of atmosphere that clings like an unclean garment to one's very soul. Yet on approaching his abode I saw, like a flicker far behind the soiled veil of the four elements, the wearisome and splendid glitter of a blue sea with the Seven Islets like minute specks swimming in my eye, the high red roof of the bungalow crowning the very smallest of them all.   This visual reminiscence was profoundly disturbing.   I knocked at the door with a faltering hand.

Old Nelson (or Nielsen) got up from the table at which he was sitting with a shabby pocket-book full of papers before him.   He took off his spectacles before shaking hands.   For a moment neither of us said a word; then, noticing me looking round somewhat expectantly, he murmured some words, of which I caught only "daughter" and "Hongkong," cast his eyes down and sighed.

His moustache, sticking all ways out, as of yore, was quite white now.   His old cheeks were softly rounded, with some colour in them; strangely enough, that something childlike always noticeable in the general contour of his physiognomy had become much more marked.   Like his handwriting, he looked childish and senile.   He showed his age most in his unintelligently furrowed, anxious forehead and in his round, innocent eyes, which appeared to me weak and blinking and watery; or was it that they were full of tears?   . . .

To discover old Nelson fully informed upon any matter whatever was a new experience.   And after the first awkwardness had worn off he talked freely, with, now and then, a question to start him going whenever he lapsed into silence, which he would do suddenly, clasping his hands on his waistcoat in an attitude which would recall to me the east verandah, where he used to sit talking quietly and puffing out his cheeks in what seemed now old, very old days.   He talked in a reasonable, somewhat anxious tone.

"No, no.   We did not know anything for weeks. Out of the way like that, we couldn't, of course.   No mail service to the Seven Isles.   But one day I ran over to Banka in my big sailing-boat to see whether there

were any letters, and saw a Dutch paper. But it
looked only like a bit of marine news: English brig
Bonito gone ashore outside Makassar roads. That was
all. I took the paper home with me and showed it to
her. 'I will never forgive him!' she cries with her old
spirit. 'My dear,' I said, 'you are a sensible girl.
The best man may lose a ship. But what about your
health?' I was beginning to be frightened at her
looks. She would not let me talk even of going to
Singapore before. But, really, such a sensible girl
couldn't keep on objecting for ever. 'Do what you
like, papa,' she says. Rather a job, that. Had to
catch a steamer at sea, but I got her over all right.
There, doctors, of course. Fever. Anæmia. Put her
to bed. Two or three women very kind to her. Naturally in our papers the whole story came out before long.
She reads it to the end, lying on the couch; then hands
the newspaper back to me, whispers 'Heemskirk,' and
goes off into a faint.''

He blinked at me for quite a long time, his eyes
running full of tears again.

"Next day," he began, without any emotion in his
voice, "she felt stronger, and we had a long talk. She
told me everything."

Here old Nelson, with his eyes cast down, gave me
the whole story of the Heemskirk episode in Freya's
words; then went on in his rather jerky utterance, and
looking up innocently:

"'My dear,' I said, 'you have behaved in the main
like a sensible girl.' 'I have been horrid,' she cries,
'and he is breaking his heart over there.' Well, she
was too sensible not to see she wasn't in a state to
travel. But I went. She told me to go. She was
being looked after very well. Anæmia. Getting better
they said."

He paused.

"You did see him?" I murmured.

"Oh, yes; I did see him," he started again, talking in that reasonable voice as though he were arguing a point. "I did see him. I came upon him. Eyes sunk an inch into his head; nothing but skin on the bones of his face, a skeleton in dirty white clothes. That's what he looked like. How Freya . . . But she never did—not really. He was sitting there, the only live thing for miles along that coast, on a drift-log washed up on the shore. They had clipped his hair in the hospital, and it had not grown again. He stared, holding his chin in his hand, and with nothing on the sea between him and the sky but that wreck. When I came up to him he just moved his head a bit. 'Is that you, old man?' says he—like that.

"If you had seen him you would have understood at once how impossible it was for Freya to have ever loved that man. Well, well. I don't say. She might have—something. She was lonely, you know. But really to go away with him! Never! Madness. She was too sensible . . . I began to reproach him gently. And by and by he turns on me. 'Write to you! What about? Come to her! What with? If I had been a man I would have carried her off, but she made a child, a happy child, of me. Tell her that the day the only thing I had belonging to me in the world perished on this reef I discovered that I had no power over her. . . . Has she come here with you?' he shouts, blazing at me suddenly with his hollow eyes. I shook my head. Come with me, indeed! Anæmia! 'Aha! You see? Go away, then, old man, and leave me alone here with that ghost,' he says, jerking his head at the wreck of his brig.

"Mad! It was getting dusk. I did not care to stop

any longer all by myself with that man in that lonely place. I was not going to tell him of Freya's illness. Anæmia! What was the good? Mad! And what sort of husband would he have made, anyhow, for a sensible girl like Freya? Why, even my little property I could not have left them. The Dutch authorities would never have allowed an Englishman to settle there. It was not sold then. My man Mahmat, you know, was looking after it for me. Later on I let it go for a tenth of its value to a Dutch half-caste. But never mind. It was nothing to me then. Yes; I went away from him. I caught the return mail-boat. I told everything to Freya. 'He's mad,' I said; 'and, my dear, the only thing he loved was his brig.'

"'Perhaps,' she says to herself, looking straight away—her eyes were nearly as hollow as his—'perhaps it is true. Yes! I would never allow him any power over me.'"

Old Nelson paused. I sat fascinated, and feeling a little cold in that room with a blazing fire.

"So you see," he continued, "she never really cared for him. Much too sensible. I took her away to Hongkong. Change of climate, they said. Oh, those doctors! My God! Winter time! There came ten days of cold mists and wind and rain. Pneumonia. But look here! We talked a lot together. Days and evenings. Who else had she? . . . She talked a lot to me, my own girl. Sometimes she would laugh a little. Look at me and laugh a little——"

I shuddered. He looked up vaguely, with a childish, puzzled moodiness.

"She would say: 'I did not really mean to be a bad daughter to you, papa.' And I would say: 'Of course, my dear. You could not have meant it.' She would lie quiet and then say: 'I wonder?' And sometimes,

'I've been really a coward,' she would tell me. You know, sick people they say things. And so she would say too: 'I've been conceited, headstrong, capricious. I sought my own gratification. I was selfish or afraid.' . . . But sick people, you know, they say anything. And once, after lying silent almost all day, she said: 'Yes; perhaps, when the day came I would not have gone. Perhaps! I don't know,' she cried. 'Draw the curtain, papa. Shut the sea out. It reproaches me with my folly.'" He gasped and paused.

"So you see," he went on in a murmur. "Very ill, very ill indeed. Pneumonia. Very sudden." He pointed his finger at the carpet, while the thought of the poor girl, vanquished in her struggle with three men's absurdities, and coming at last to doubt her own self, held me in a very anguish of pity.

"You see yourself," he began again in a downcast manner. "She could not have really . . . She mentioned you several times. Good friend. Sensible man. So I wanted to tell you myself—let you know the truth. A fellow like that! How could it be? She was lonely. And perhaps for a while . . . Mere nothing. There could never have been a question of love for my Freya—such a sensible girl——"

"Man!" I cried, rising upon him wrathfully, "don't you see that she died of it?"

He got up too. "No! no!" he stammered, as if angry. "The doctors! Pneumonia. Low state. The inflammation of the . . . They told me. Pneu——"

He did not finish the word. It ended in a sob. He flung his arms out in a gesture of despair, giving up his ghastly pretence with a low, heartrending cry:

"And I thought that she was so sensible!"

THE END